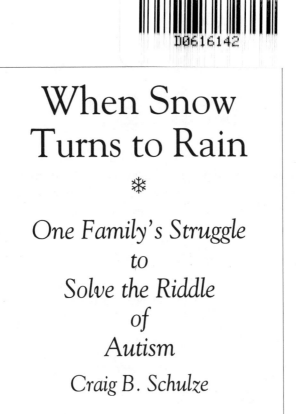

When Snow Turns to Rain

❆

One Family's Struggle
to
Solve the Riddle
of
Autism

Craig B. Schulze

WOODBINE HOUSE ❆ 1993

Published by:
Woodbine House
5615 Fishers Lane
Rockville, MD 20852
800/843–7323

Cover photography: Linda Bartlett

Library of Congress Cataloging-in-Publication Data

Schulze, Craig B.
    When snow turns to rain : one family's struggle to solve the
riddle of autism / by Craig B. Schulze.
        p.   cm.
    ISBN 0–933149–63–8 (pbk.) : $14.95
    1. Schulze, Jordan, 1982–   —Mental health. 2. Autistic
children—United States—Biography. 3. Autistic children—
United States—Family relationships. 4. Schulze,
Craig B.—Family   I. Title.
RJ506.A9S42   1993
618.92'689'820092—dc20
[B]   93–10209
                                                        CIP

Manufactured in the United States of America

10 9 8 7 6 5 4 3 2 1

Prologue

*O*n a bitter, moonless night in mid-December, I am standing at my bedroom window in Acton, Massachusetts, peering
out across our backyard to the street just beyond. The scene is
vaguely illuminated by the reflections of the street lamps and
Christmas lights off the densely packed snow. It is a night
whose stillness invites reflection, and, at this invitation, my
thoughts are a blend of the past, present, and future.

It is small wonder that I should think of the past at this
moment, for my present gaze intersects the path that the
Minutemen from this town took on their way to join their em-
battled compatriots at the North Bridge in 1775. A small
stone marker a little way up the street commemorates the
event in dignified understatement, like so much of the
colonial history in this area of the country. As for the present,
it, too, reverberates with the theme of liberty in this year,
1989, when Communism is falling like lines of redcoats
around the capitals of Eastern Europe. And the future seems
to hold even brighter prospects for worldwide democracy and
freedom.

But at this watershed period in history, my thoughts are
not about the triumphs and travails of liberty. I am haunted
by more personal apparitions of the past, present, and future.
The Christmas lights from the neighbor's house bring to mind
a Yuletide season just a half dozen years back. A clear-eyed
boy of nineteen months is pointing to the gaily decorated tree
in my living room. "Christmas lights, Daddy," he says as he
reaches up to touch the bulbs. "This one is green. This one is
blue." Jordan goes through all the colors, carefully pointing
out the names of each that he touches. From across the room
my wife, Jill, beams as she listens to these first words of the
season from our first child.

I am not long in this reverie when the second of the season's ghosts intrudes on my consciousness. It is a vision of what has occurred only a few hours ago. I see my wife and daughter pulling up to my in-laws' house in Columbia, Maryland. They are tired and irritable, having spent over seven hours in the car on their monthly trek south. Tomorrow, Jill will start a two-week stint of work as a lawyer for Maryland's Attorney General's office. When she returns to Acton in two weeks, she will bring along a stack of files to complete her month's work at home. This is the arrangement that we cobbled together four months ago when we moved to Massachusetts. Wearing as this routine is, it enables us to live in Massachusetts while Jill keeps her job in Maryland. More importantly, it enables our son to be a day, rather than residential, student at Boston Higashi School, where he has matriculated for the past two years. Jordan has autism.

The boy who marveled at the Christmas tree and the mute boy sleeping in the next room are one and the same, though the vision of that happier past and the one that my mind is playing back of this evening seem to come from two different worlds. The here-and-now version of the happy toddler is the seven-year-old boy who, on this day alone, has bitten the school bus driver, flung himself on the floor in a fit of rage in the grocery store, spent nearly half an hour tapping toys on his teeth, and occupied himself in his last waking hour flushing the toilet over twenty times.

Over the past five years there have been slight variations on this theme, but the pattern has been basically the same— rituals of repetition, wild mood swings, episodic aggression, and abnormal compulsions surrounding objects and activities. These behaviors and other traits, such as difficulty with communication and self-stimulatory actions, are characteristic of people with autism. And their bizarre behavior is made to seem even more peculiar by the fact that they usually appear physically normal.

As I ponder this grotesque disorder, other realities of the present wash over my brain. I am thirty-nine years old and unemployed; currently on a second leave of absence from my job as a school administrator in Baltimore. I have been unable to find similar work in Massachusetts, and prospects of my ever doing so seem slim at best. At the end of this year, Jill and I will have to choose among three options: to stay in Massachusetts under our current arrangement; to have Jill quit her job in Maryland and join me in a search for work here; or to move back to Maryland where there seems to be no appropriate day school for Jordan. This picture of the present seems uncertain, but the ghost who represents the future is the scariest of all. For he brings visions of an older Jordan—increasingly isolated, dysfunctional, and aggressive, living in an institution. He shows me a family financially strapped and emotionally drained from years of dealing with a difficult child. And he reminds me of the most frightening element of all—that the power to alter any of these outcomes may be completely beyond my control.

I quake a little at these thoughts and slump down on the edge of my bed. I realize I need to exorcize these ghosts. Somehow I must go back to the beginning of Jordan's life and retrace the steps; run the gauntlet of retelling. I walk out into the dark hallway and down toward the living room. From the bookshelf I pick up the two diaries that we kept of the first three years of Jordan's life. They feel cold to the touch as I squeeze them together in the palm of my hand. I return to the bedroom and place the diaries on my bureau. Slipping under the icy sheets, I resolve to begin the long journey back in the morning.

I

*F*rom the sixteenth floor of Baltimore's Mercy Hospital I watch the heavy snow fall leaden toward the street below. On its rapid descent to the ground it seems to change to rain, creating a glistening sheen that smiles up from the sidewalk to brighten an otherwise dull day. As I gaze out the window, I chuckle at this "snowstorm in May" birth story I will one day share with the child about to be born.

Now, though, the obstetrician recalls me from these thoughts with a reminder that there is work yet to be done before the advent of the blessed event. The heavy contractions are coming at regular intervals, and my help is needed with the breathing and the subsequent pushing stage. A surging sea of emotions is rising within me. Soon I will face my firstborn.

A short time afterward, I am poking this tiny vessel of protoplasm perched upon my wife's exhausted body. I have a son. We gaze long and hard at this new life before us; silent, reverential, almost oblivious to the world around. Even the doctor and the two medical students who observed the birth seem to speak to each other from another room. A crescendo has sounded deep in our souls, and the resonance from that sound holds us in its rapture long into the afternoon.

While all of this is happening, a part of me seems to stand outside the scene observing the participants, wondering how it is possible that this life has come to be mine: a twentieth century American birth, a good education, a satisfying career, financial security, a happy and stable marriage of ten years, and now the birth of this healthy child. Realizing that such a small percentage of humanity experiences such life circumstances, I am chastened.

Why am I so fortunate? I do not believe in a personal God, and I cannot name the invisible hand that has placed me so well. Yet, thanksgiving for these blessings pours from me like a cataract. These are the thoughts that come to me in the bonding hours.

As if fate hasn't been kind enough, the child we call Jordan is born on May 19th—late spring. I have squirreled away enough sick and personal leave from my job as an elementary school teacher to be home with Jill and the baby until the beginning of June. Then, I will have only a couple of weeks left before the school year comes to a close. From the middle of June until the beginning of September, I will be home with my family. Hallowed be thy—whatever. ❄

❄

❄

❄

❄ The summer passes so quickly. As with many first-time parents, we become absorbed with our child, and, because we have so much time to spend with him, the absorption becomes an obsession. We take pictures, make movies, keep a diary of his progress. Each event in his young life is duly recorded; his first smile, his first illness, his first reaction to music, his first attempt to grasp for a toy. All of it is there for posterity. Neither he nor we will have to invent or imagine his past.

In the early days there are postpartum stresses, to be sure, but the ease of caring for this tranquil baby extends the ethereal quality of our lives into the summer and beyond. Long, leisurely days provide opportunities for us to take walks, exercise, read, listen to music, garden, and cultivate our relationships. We are at one with each other and the universe.

Early in August I learn that I'm to be promoted to a supervisory position. This means that I will no longer be facing the sixty-hour work weeks that come with the territory of teaching first grade. It also means that I will probably be able to complete the Ph.D. program I have been listlessly pursuing for the past six years. The upcoming school year will be a busy one, but at least I will have been relieved of much of the grunt work. Another piece of the puzzle falls into place.

As fall approaches, and Jill and I must return to work, we worry about child care arrangements. Horror stories about day care abuse abound, and we remain concerned that, even under the best of circumstances, some unforeseen cataclysm could result from Jordan receiving his primary care from someone other than his parents. Here again divine intervention appears to save the day. A complex arrangement involving the use of relatives, friends, and child care exchange is jerry-rigged to meet our baby sitting needs. The schedule elicits the proverbial "If it's Tuesday this must be . . ." comments, but we have a "staff" we trust implicitly, and everything goes well. We stagger our work hours to reduce the amount of time that Jordan must spend with each sitter, all of whom are quick to point out what we sense from our evenings with him—that he is doing just fine without us.

Although a somewhat smallish baby at birth (6 pounds, 7 ounces), Jordan puts on weight quickly. He also remains relatively free of illness. His days seem to have a balance about them, with active and passive periods, curiosity as well as blank stares, and contentedness interspersed with times of distress. He nurses easily from the start and sleeps through the night by eight weeks. Throughout the first year of his life Jordan remains a happy, healthy, and, as far as anyone can determine, normal baby. The early developmental milestones are met on time or ahead of schedule. Smiling, babbling, crawling, playing interactive games, and the development of receptive language proceed apace. Jill's entry from our diary is illustrative.

> *December 16, 1982 and January 5, 1983*
>
> Jordan can discriminate the names of several objects and looks at the appropriate person when asked, "Where's Mommy or Daddy?" He is also showing heightened interest in books, especially such classics as **I Am a Bunny.** Additionally, he is crawling in a classic four-legged style now, and getting all over in his walker, even on the shag rug.
>
> Despite his current cold, he is very pleasant and happy, and our intense love for him continues to grow.

In terms of physical development, Jordan seems ahead of the game. It takes him, for instance, only about the same amount of time that he spent in the womb to begin to take his first steps once out. He is still a little on the small side, and it seems incredible to watch this child, standing only slightly higher than my knee, maneuver bipedally. Now the house is his. Seeing how quickly he exhausts the available space of our tiny Cape Cod makes us confident that our plan to move to a bigger house with a larger yard is the right thing to do despite concerns about the financial impact.

Just before spring we find the perfect place, a three-bedroom rancher on a cul-de-sac with an acre of ground that backs up to state park land. Amazingly, it is only a mile from the main access route into Baltimore, so neither Jill nor I will have more than a half-hour commute to work.

Even before we have settled on the place, we draw up plans for improving it. A screened-in porch utilizing half of the carport would give us an extra room in summer. A deck

off the back of the porch would be a wonderful spot for surveying our land by day or the canopy of stars by night. An outdoor fireplace at the end of a new patio would make dinners
during warm weather seasons convenient and fun. The ideas
fly like the finches that swoop down, nesting materials in
beak, into the thicket behind the site of our new garden.

Spring is on the land. The car pulls away from the
driveway and begins its ascent up the steep incline from our
courtyard. In the rear-view mirror I catch a final glimpse of
the rows of red and violet azaleas that form a gateway to our
new house. I have my hand on Jill's leg, and I want to squeeze
it like I want to squeeze every moment out of this wonderful
month of May, 1983.

Jill reminds me that my immediate mission is to ensure
the family's safe return from this visit to what will soon be our
new house. I get hold of myself, but only temporarily, as I jerk
the mirror down a notch so I can look at Jordan. A little
peanut of a kid, he is dwarfed in his carseat; yet, he has been
walking for over two months and has already learned, what
seems to us, a tremendous amount. And he hasn't reached his
first birthday. Jill summarizes the state of things at the end of
Jordan's first year:

> *May 11, 1983*
>
> *Our lives are so good that it scares us—seems like
> something has to go wrong. We love our boy so much,
> and he seems to enjoy us, too. Nearly every night we take
> a walk in the Woodlawn Cemetery. Jordan loves riding in
> the backpack, and I can always elicit a smile as I walk
> alongside or jog by.*
>
> *Jordan understands much of what we say to him,
> especially, "Do you want to. . .*
> *read a book?"*
> *have some milk?"*
> *take a bath?"*

> *Those questions invoke a smile and a "hoohoo." He*
> *also enjoys being chased and chasing us around the house.*
> *He now says Daddy, ditcha (picture), tock (clock), and*
> *Mama, which is often said while clinging to my leg.*

In the final week before our move, we set up Jordan's first birthday party in the twenty or so square feet not covered by boxes packed with our stuff. Our friends and neighbors of the past ten years walk down from their house to help us celebrate. It is a bittersweet occasion, as we recognize that we'll no longer have the easy access to each other that we've enjoyed for so long.

Despite our regrets, we are happy in our new home. Before long another summer approaches, bringing with it both opportunities and decisions. Specifically, I am offered a curriculum-writing position that would give me greater involvement in shaping, on a much broader scale, what kids are taught. It is an attractive offer that I don't turn down lightly, but Jill and I agree that it is more important for Jordan to have a couple of months with a full-time parent. This plan will also buy us more time to provide a more coherent child care situation in the fall, our old arrangement having been rendered almost unworkable by the move. There isn't much arm twisting required here, as I look forward to watching our little toddler grow.

And the days pass in a harvest of rapid development. New verbal, cognitive, social, and physical skills appear daily.

July 5th and 10th, 1983

> *Currently, Jordan has about 15 words with which he*
> *can correctly respond to the question, "Who, or what, is*
> *this?" Among these are door, tea, stick, pot, clock, car,*
> *tree, dog, book, sock, teeth, and apple. Lately, he will go*
> *around and say the names of these things as he touches*
> *them.*

When he is being read to, he frequently calls out the names of objects that he recognizes.

He has several new physical skills as well. He can get himself seated in his chair, hit a toy nail with his workbench hammer, roll a truck across the floor, and "dance" to music.

In this second summer with Jordan I am more at ease than ever. Aside from a number of ear infections, a problem which we hope is solved by the insertion of drainage tubes just after his first birthday, Jordan is rarely slowed down. He seems to be constantly moving and exploring, yet he seldom endangers himself. Best of all, he, like me, loves being outdoors. Thus, I'm free to enjoy my garden and the land around it for much of the day, while delighting in the company of this still bald little playmate.

In a typical memory from that summer I see Jordan rushing toward the kitchen door and banging it with his little hand. "Side!" he yells at a decibel level that catches my attention. "Come on, Jord, it's about 95 degrees out there," I plead. But my entreaties fail to dissuade the little guy from his desire to run amok around the backyard. Once the door is grudgingly opened, he doesn't bother to wait for his dad but takes off like a shot for the garden, stopping only to smell a couple of flowers and to pick up a stick. I follow behind and watch him practically roll down the steep incline leading to the vegetable patch. As he reaches the edge of the garden, he actually does trip, and he crushes a pepper plant in the fall. Before I make it there to see if he's O.K., he is up and inspecting the damage.

"Pap," he says, looking at the one pepper that made it to maturity before the plant's untimely death.

"Yeah," I respond. "That's a pepper, and we might have had a few more of them if we didn't have a monkey like you to deal with." I swoop down on him like a hawk and toss him as high in the air as I can. He squeals with delight and collapses into delirium as I roll him around in the grass. When he catches his breath, he gets quiet, and I lie down beside him. He touches my beard and looks long into my face, seeming to have received the promise of love that I send through my eyes.

August 1, 1983

Gracious! A new month is upon us, and half the summer is gone. Slowly, but surely, Jordan increases his receptive and expressive language. He can say perhaps sixty words and understands at least twice that many.

Although at times tedious and stressful, being a day-care daddy has had many positive moments. Typically, Jordan has been active, happy, curious, and a horribly messy eater. More than anything else, I have been impressed with his memory. Not infrequently, he remembers words or the location of objects over a fairly long period of time, even when he has had only a single exposure.

As this dreamy summer is about to draw to a close, we receive word that my father has throat cancer and will be operated on within days. On the night I am to drive to my parents' house in New Jersey, we sit in the kitchen eating dinner. Jill bends over Jordan and attempts to wipe his face with the tiny spot on the bib that remains clean after the meal. Seeing the folly of this effort, I suggest that she let the gunk stay caked on him until bath time, pointing out that she's sure to discover new and unexpected locations of dried food once she inspects him in his birthday suit. My comments don't elicit the usual animated response this evening, though. In truth, neither of us is very spirited tonight.

It was twenty years ago that my father's father learned he had lung and throat cancer, and the thought of his final years—the radiation treatments, the special diet, the visible agony, and the final demise at his own hands by shotgun blast—are with me tonight. I comfort myself with the knowledge that the treatments are more sophisticated now than they were in 1963, but the realities are that Dad was a heavy smoker who lived and worked around hazardous materials for the balance of his life, and I'm not optimistic. Ironically, it has only been in the last couple of years that he and I have developed a good relationship. Now I wonder what I can possibly say to help him or my mother.

Later that evening I arrive at my parents' house to find my mother surprisingly upbeat. What's more, I'm told that Dad is also expressing a positive attitude. I tell myself, "The doctors have been pumping them with the same 'high-tech high-hopes' dreams that I have been feeding on for the past few days. Reality is liable to be something altogether different."

But after the surgery, there seems genuine reason for optimism. The cancer was pretty extensive, but the doctors believe that they've gotten it all, and, only hours after the operation, Dad is gripping my arm with a strength that recalls the days of my childhood, when that vice-like grip was applied as a corrective for various acts of mischief. It will be a long time before he will eat or talk normally, but Dad is in uncharacteristically good spirits, and at the family post-operative briefing at Mom's later on, everyone counts the operation a success. Much of our worry allayed, the talk turns to Grandma's eightieth birthday and the plans for the surprise party. We're all excited about the prospect of having four generations and the four great-grandchildren together, not to mention seeing cousins and kids of cousins we rarely see.

By morning my two brothers have packed and gone. I stay on only the rest of the afternoon, seeing that my mother no longer needs me. Shortly after dinner I am on my way. As I pass over the Delaware Memorial Bridge and gaze down at the river, a plume of fetid air envelops the car. It is a sauna of an August night that makes it hard to think about anything other than the air conditioned living room that awaits me in Ellicott City. While the car moves my dream state along, I wonder how the last two days have gone at home. Jordan was to have spent his first full sessions with the new babysitter, a naturalized American citizen from Colombia who, though a resident of this country for nearly twenty years, still speaks with a noticeable accent. That accent and her overprotective manner with her own son worry us a little, but she seems to really love Jordan, and, in his initial contacts with her, everything goes fine.

I fly over the bump into the driveway and pull the car to a stop. My sticky body peels like velcro as I detach myself from the vinyl seat. I'm so hot that I leave the car unpacked and rush into the house for a beer and an update. The oppressive heat notwithstanding, all is well. Jill is convinced that this year's child care arrangements will work out. That's good, because tomorrow I go back to work. Jordan's development continues on schedule, as Jill's report at sixteen months reveals:

September 19, 1983

Here is an update of Jordan's progress at sixteen months. He walks, runs, tumbles, and wrestles. He likes to play "catch Jordan" (he gets chased or does the chasing), "who's got the ball?", and "peekaboo"—behind pillows or through holes.

He calls me Mama and usually pats my head or chest while doing so. He selects books by name and whines as he casts aside a disfavored book chosen by a parent who has read a favorite too many times that day.

On our very frequent hikes in the park, he identifies moss, dirt, road, rock, tree, leaf and log. He sometimes even says "big tree."

A couple of times in the last three days or so he's asked for "more juice." And he loves wearing his "mocksins," and grins at the thought of putting them on. He is also beginning to be able to identify some letters. He can usually identify O, T and B, and sometimes gets I and Z.

He seems to be quite happy at the babysitter's, particularly when Stephen [the sitter's six-year-old son] is home from school. All in all, he is a very pleasant, happy boy with very little fear of strangers and a good disposition. Nearly everyone can win a smile. ❄

❄

❄

❄

❄ It seems a wonderful and perhaps universal disposition of the human spirit, especially among children, to be able to find beauty even in the most antagonistic of circumstances. Growing up a working-class child in Camden, New Jersey, I had very few opportunities to experience beauty, especially that most fundamental of beauties, the majesty of nature. Yet I remember a number of events and objects from my surroundings that impressed me as being beautiful. One such experience is with me today. I go back about twenty-five years to my grandmother's house. "Mom," as we called her then, is walking across the living room floor to plug in the latest addition to her decor. It is a picture made of some translucent material that displays a hillside blazing in autumnal splendor. Behind the picture is a bulb which, when lit in a dim room, makes the scene come alive. At the time, even the treasures of Louis XIV could not have compared favorably with that picture for beauty in my mind.

Now fast forward to the present, and I am observing reality's counterpart to the picture in my grandmother's living room. It is the middle of October, and I am standing at the back of my carport, looking out at the slope of deciduous trees in peak color that rises some two hundred yards away from the end of my property. So enchanting is this color show that I barely notice the racket Jordan is making puttering around with his "cornpopper." For perhaps two minutes I take in this scene, and then I pick my little boy up and direct his attention to the forest across the way. "Look, Jordan," I whisper, "so many trees." He gazes out and repeats my phrase with a fidelity that is at once gratifying and astonishing.

Throughout the fall, Jordan and I continue this ritual of looking at the trees every day when we get home from the sitter's. The glorious reds and yellows slowly fade into the bare brown branches of late November. So exquisite have the autumn colors been, that Jill and I resolve that we won't go another season without that deck and screened-in porch that we've coveted as the final piece of our dream puzzle. As luck would have it, Jill's brother, a deck builder and landscaper, is just closing out his work season. He agrees to give us the entire package of screened-in porch, deck, and outdoor fireplace for little more than cost, provided he gets the pleasure of watching me fall over myself as his assistant.

After two bone-chilling weekends of bull work, the project is finished, just in time for Thanksgiving. Two nights after the last nail is driven, Jill and I christen our "platform under the stars" with a bottle of wine and a midnight embrace. Orion creeps over the roof, and we salute him and the radiance of the past season. But we save our fondest toast for the celestial visitation whose presence has cast a brilliant light on our lives for the past eighteen months. Again, Jill captures Jordan's unfolding progress:

November 25, 1983

*The day after Thanksgiving and we woke up to a
heavy snowfall. It didn't amount to much, but it did
provide a fascinated boy with a real life illustration of a
phenomenon he has seen in books. He quickly caught on.
Jordan also put five words together to form a sentence this
morning: "Down the hill big pole."*

*Jordan knows several colors now including blue,
green, purple, orange, red and yellow. He also knows the
entire alphabet, though he misses one or two occasionally.*

*This morning I was thrilled when he asked me to give
him a hug: another first.* ❋

❋

❋

❋

❋ "'Twas the night before Christmas and all through the
_____,"

"House."

"Not a creature was stirring, not even a _____,"

"Mouse."

We proceed this way through the entire poem, and Jordan
supplies the correct ending for each line. He's heard this book
maybe four or five times, and now it's committed to memory.
But it seems more than just memorization of the sounds. If I
show him a picture of Santa Claus, for example, and ask him
to show me his boots, he is 100 percent reliable to point out
the boots. Moreover, if I ask him to show me Jordan's boots,
he can go to the closet and pick them out. I scratch my head
in disbelief. Five months ago he could say maybe fifteen
words, and now he knows the names of well over a hundred

things plus many adjectives and verbs as well. What's more, he speaks with almost perfect clarity.

As far as Jill and I are concerned, the vocabulary development piece is fine, but the real jewel in the crown is Jordan's disposition. He is almost never inexplicably fussy; he goes down easily at bed time and for naps; he eats well; he follows directions; and he is very affectionate. He seems particularly happy during this holiday season, exhibiting delight at the sight of the candles, trimmings, and Christmas tree, which he frequently asks to have turned on. His infectious nature makes our Christmas an extraordinary time as well.

These holidays pass in a blur; a dizzying final rush to the end of what has seemed a year-long peak experience. I struggle to come up with the proper image to describe the year as Jill and I get dressed for a New Year's Eve party. Thinking back to my college statistics course, I settle on the prosaic "statistical outlier" as the most apt characterization of 1983. Yes, that's it! If you plotted my emotional life on an axis, with the years gone by on the horizontal and the amount of happiness I experienced on the vertical, 1983 would stand alone on the top of the graph, looking down at a series of points, which if connected, would form a relatively straight line parallel to the horizontal axis. But this isn't the time for daydreaming. Jill shakes me from my mathematical musings with a reminder that dawdling could keep us from securing first dibs on Debra's hors d'oeuvres.

At the party there is much talk about entering that terrifying year of 1984. Our theatrical hostess insists on each of us sharing something of our hopes and expectations for the coming year. For a crowd used to getting a steady diet of cynicism and malcontent from the group's only nonlawyer, it must seem something of a Pollyanna-like apostasy to hear me suggest that it would be just marvelous if 1984, and every year thereafter for that matter, could simply be an extension of the year just passed. In fact, all present agree that, if we could only close our eyes to the fate of the overwhelming majority of humanity, we just might be living in the best of times.

Our eyes and glasses meet against a backdrop of "Hear, hears!" We move gracefully back to our seats as if they were the deck chairs of some long ago luxury liner and we were the passengers relaxing and taking in the view of the endless sea before us. Our vessel is impregnable against the ice. ❄

❄

❄

❄

❄ In the evening, two days later, the phone rings. "Can you get that?" Jill calls from the kitchen.

"Darn! Why does the phone always ring at dinner time? Yeah, sure, I got it," I whiningly reply.

"Hello. Yes, I remember you—from the wedding. What's that? Good God!" I tremble as this cousin of a good friend explains that our friend died of a heart attack on New Year's Day. To make matters worse, it happened in the presence of his wife and two young children while on a drive in the family car. Amazing! Our first phone call in this allegedly ominous year brings news of the death of a close friend. A thin, active, vital man of just thirty-three years is gone in virtually an instant. This friend, who once was our downstairs neighbor and frequent companion, who was uniformly buoyant, who had the multiple talents of a Renaissance man, and who, more than anyone else we knew, seemed to celebrate life, is taken from it without the slightest warning.

For a while we are consumed with the senselessness of this event. Yet, this reminder of life's fragility and capriciousness stays with us for only a short time. The pressures of work, the joys of watching a young child develop, and the care and attention of a loving spouse place a distance between you and the bugaboo of fate. Life goes on.

> *January 16, 1984 (ironically, the entry for this date is listed 1983)*
>
> *Jordan's accelerated language and concept development is a thing of beauty. Right now he is running from the dining room to the kitchen displaying his "flashcards" (numbers, letters and words). After saying "Mommy," "6," or whatever, he returns to the dining room to get another letter.*
>
> *Yesterday, he walked around the house holding and alternately saying "dump" and "Mommy" (words from stories that have been read to him recently). It was a trick with real comic value for the visiting relatives. He also charmed the crowd by supplying the final word from various lines in books that were read to him.*
>
> *Recently, many physical activities have provided Jordan with amusement, including rolling objects of all sorts, sitting on and pushing his riding toys and taking off and putting back on lids. These skills offer him other opportunities to use expressive language. For example, when he rolls baskets, balls, or lids, he often tells his father to "catch it, daddy." Or when he makes a particularly good grab on an object rolled his way, he may remark, "Yea, Jordan!" When someone stops pushing him on a riding toy he will frequently say, "Do it again," or "One more time."*

I emerge from the basement soaked with sweat. It's been a cold and rainy stretch of weather, and I've become a fair weather jogger, resorting to what Jill affectionately calls "basement hopping,"—running around the perimeter of our ground floor family room for a period of thirty minutes. I reach for the phone to call my in-laws to alert them that I'll be over to pick up Jordan as soon as I've showered. Before I've dialed, Jill comes through the door—home early from work. She informs me that she has already spoken to Carol and Kabe and has responded affirmatively to their dinner invitation.

"Great, dessert without guilt," I chortle, poking her in the ribs.

"You might want to be a little bit careful with that," she retorts. I think I know what's coming next, but her facial expression and tone of voice seem out of keeping with the announcement I expect. "I'm pregnant again, Craig," Jill finally lets out after a pause that's as pregnant as she. There is genuine apprehension here, so I don't try to get cute. I think I can guess her primary concern. Ever since we got into the "family" business, we have been something of disciples of Burton White, who has suggested that things generally go better in a family when the kids are spaced three years apart. This little one will be born before Jordan is two and a half, so we're a little bit off in our planning. When I attempt to flesh the anxiety out further, however, I find that this is only part of the worry; there is more.

"Honey, I'm not sure I could ever love any child the way I love Jordan," she says with a look demonstrative of the obvious thought she has given the issue. It's not an idea I would have independently arrived at, but once it's put to me this way I must admit that it doesn't sound all that irrational. After some further deliberation, however, we more or less come to the conclusion that Jordan would actually benefit from a little more sharing of attention and that he would be much happier as he got older having a readily available playmate. Already I get dreams of two little boys shooting hoops and playing catch in the backyard with their old man, or the alternative thrill of having a daughter. ❄

❄

❄

❄

❄ Jill props her feet up on Jordan's vacant chair. "Any green out there yet?" she asks, noticing that I'm staring out the kitchen window into our backyard.

"No," I sigh, "everything is as bare as it was in December. But it sure will be a sight from here when the buds come out, not to mention when the trees start to flower." Just as the days leading up to Christmas morning seem interminable to a small child, so this winter period has seemed to go on forever for us.

From across the kitchen a basket lid rolls out from under the table and strikes me on the heel. I turn around in time to receive a belated invitation to "catch it, Daddy." Maybe because this gets a laugh from his parents, Jordan proceeds to roll all of the rings from his stacking toy at me. From a distance of about twelve feet, he positions each of the seven rings and sets them off on a journey that will end with each either hitting or going between my feet. No mean accomplishment for a child under two. But we see Jordan's proclivity to roll things as more than a skill; we also recognize it as something of an obsession. Because he is learning, happy, and willing to do other things, though, we downplay the compulsive quality of this and other similar behaviors and chalk it up to his "exploring the environment."

When Jordan finally loses interest in the rollathon, he heads back into the living room to look at his books. Shortly afterwards he's standing at the picture window shouting,

"Jim's blue truck!" It's his way of announcing the arrival of Jill's brother, a great favorite with the toddler set. Throughout his stay, Jim is badgered to perform a variety of lifting and tossing exercises that will provide Jordan with that brush with danger he so craves. Only after obvious exhaustion sets in does Jim decline to continue the game. That refusal sets off some imploring gestures and a few unanswered whines, but eventually Jordan gives up. And, as usual, no temper tantrum emerges, so the adults are free to get on with their conversation.

Later on, after Jordan has been put to bed, we hear him saying to himself, "Jim's blue truck," "catch it, Daddy," and other words and phrases he has used during the day. Hearing these things said out of context seems strange and a little bit eerie, but what are we to make of it? We tell ourselves that he is practicing his language, and there the matter ends.

With Jordan's second birthday approaching, Jill writes this entry in the diary:

> *March 4, 1984*
>
> *Jordan is speaking in full sentences: "I see a great big tree"; "I want a cracker"; etc. He has also started using "please" as an implorative. He absolutely refuses to eat vegetables unless they have "sauce" on them. He requires only a minute touch of barbecue sauce, but an absence of said is unfailingly detected.*
>
> *Jordan is very affectionate and loves to give and receive hugs and kisses. He greatly endears himself to his grandparents by asking to hug them and insisting on kissing them when they say good-bye.*
>
> *He loves to roll objects and is much more proficient at it than any adults who try to match him. He also loves to run and dance and often dances about in sheer excitement. He still knows the letters of the alphabet, numbers, and colors, but we have decided against pursuing teaching him any more sight words.*

> *Overall, at 21 months: happy, good disposition, good*
> *appetite, great language and memory, and rather poor*
> *sleeper (only eight or nine hours a night).*

April in Ellicott City, Maryland! Is it any better in Paris?
I think not. It turns out that I was right about the dogwood
and the redbud in the forest behind our house. In fact, I greatly underestimated the variety and beauty of the trees available
for viewing from the deck. There are crabapples, apples, wil-
lows, and more. In a giddy moment while surveying them, I
commit myself to taking a picture of this scene, having it
mounted on translucent material and placing it in a frame
with a bulb. A nice eighty-fifth birthday present for Grandma
Millie.

It's twilight, and I'm putting in another row of beans. The
air is a mixture of scents, the humus from the freshly turned
earth, the pungent cuttings from the just-mowed lawn, the
faint aroma of flowering trees wafting down from the hillside,
and the subtle, almost numinous, smell of rejuvenation. From
the deck, Jill calls down to express her appreciation for all the
work I've done this afternoon. She offers the season's first iced
tea and some cookies that she and Jordan have baked as a
reward for my efforts. I'm a lazy gardener and am easily
tempted away from my proper responsibility of getting in that
last row of beans. As I pack up the gardening grip, I take a
final surmise of the land. This year's harvest should be even
better than last.

I enter the house through the basement, take off my
grimy clothes, and climb the stairs that lead into the kitchen.
There I find a neatly stacked plate of oatmeal cookies and a
tall glass of iced tea. The air is still warm and sweet outside, so
I decide to enjoy the final moments of daylight from the
screened-in porch, running the risk of having a neighbor
come upon me in the buff. Lying on the couch there, I hear

Jordan singing in the bath. The tune and lyrics are unmistakably "Twinkle, Twinkle, Little Star," one of the several
songs he has learned in the past few weeks. It is a soft and fitting lullaby for this sultry spring evening and is sung with a
fidelity which belies his tender age. While enjoying the
serenade, I ponder the things that Jordan has learned—the
songs, the alphabet, colors, numbers, shapes, his address,
telephone numbers, answers to questions such as "who's the
President?" and others. It seems such a prodigious amount for
a child who has not yet reached two. I sometimes think that I
am just a proud father, but relatives and friends have com-
mented on these abilities too. Is it just a fast start that will
even out in time? Could he be gifted? The term has become
repugnant to me, so often have I heard it used by parents wish-
ing to set their own child apart from others. Could it mean
that he will have a difficult time in school?

The ice is melting in the tea, and the cookies are starting
to harden. I fall back to a gentle equilibrium as the sun dies
over my neighbor's yard. ❉

❉

❉

❉

❉ "Sooner or later," I suggest in a pious tone, "when dealing with autocrats, you'll run afoul of the system for inde-
pendence of thought." Once again Jill is being subjected to
one of my almost daily diatribes against life in the big city
school bureaucracy. Having to report to two supervisors, and
being constantly pressured to undertake activities that seem to
offer little benefit to children, has made my work life considerably less than optimal recently, and, to my discredit, I've been

carrying a good bit of the baggage home. The latest tirade has been brought on by what I feel was an unjust criticism of how I use my time and has had the unheard of effect of troubling my sleep.

"If you feel like your work isn't being appreciated, why don't you look for something else?" Jill replies in a voice that shows the strain of having tired of this discussion. Her response achieves its intended effect of changing the subject. Anyway, it's getting late, and we both need the sleep. Not long after we settle into bed and turn on the news, Jill is snoring away. It will be a couple of hours before I drift off, lost as I am in thought about how to rectify my unpleasant work situation. The next day Jill wakes up not feeling right, and, as the day progresses, she starts to bleed. The doctor advises her to rest all day and not to think the worst, but by bedtime it's pretty clear that she's having a miscarriage. Throughout the night she has contraction-like pains which eventually produce the aborted fetus. It is a long, physically and emotionally painful night for Jill, and, to make matters worse, I am less than optimally supportive of her through the ordeal. The next couple of weeks are difficult, but time and the beauty of spring turn our eyes toward our blessings.

Jill's positive tone in the following entry reflects our rebound:

> *May 7, 1984*
>
> *Our depression of having lost the baby has been lightened by the presence of our boy, who now interacts with us through words and gestures and obviously enjoys it quite a bit. He will actually sit on (even climbs into) my lap and hold a conversation with me. Two stories he often asks for are "No Mouse For Me" and "I Am a Mouse," both of which are abridged versions of library books. He loves talking, games, and giving and getting hugs.*

Jordan is a thorough delight which, coupled with the joy Craig and I have in each other, is more than enough to keep our spirits high despite our loss. ❄

❄

❄

❄

❄ "Daddy play 'This Old Man'!" the call comes from the dining room, suggesting the start of another music appreciation period. I put down the newspaper and amble over to where Jordan is crashing his toy school bus into our album collection. I pull out the requested L.P. and put it on the turntable.

"Here comes Kookaburra," I announce after the initial selection has played and the next song is about to come on.

"No, no, 'This Old Man'!" Jordan protests as the next song begins to play. The album on the turntable contains perhaps twenty-five songs, but Jordan is only interested in hearing his favorite. He insists that I play it five or six times and becomes highly annoyed if I suggest any of the other tunes. Having gone through this same scenario on several other occasions recently, I begin to realize the futility of my importuning for variety. I'm a little tired, though, of playing stereo steward for Lord Fauntleroy, so I suggest that we go out to play for a while. Though slightly agitated for not getting a longer session with his "greatest hit," Jordan accepts the bait, and we're on our way out into the broiling sun. As we descend the stairs leading from the deck, he catches a glimpse of the electric meter. "Clock," he says as he cranes his neck around me to get a better view of this prized environmental stimulus. "No, that's a meter, Jordan," I instruct. "NO! Clock!" he vociferously demurs. I wisely decline to respond further and resolve to ask a friend, who will be visiting with his own two-year-old later in the day, if this is behavior he is also seeing.

When Richard and Shirley and their daughter, Jessica, arrive that afternoon, I immediately suggest that the women folk work on hustling up dinner, while the guys and the kids head for the playground. I want to isolate Richard and Shirley in order to solicit their unbiased opinions regarding the question of terrible two behavior as well as get their gut feelings on how they think Jordan is doing. When I pose the question to Richard, he seems a little surprised by my concern and submits that, among the ten or so two-year-olds he sees regularly at Jessica's playgroup, he observes many examples of a more virulent obstinacy than he has ever noticed with Jordan. And as far as Jordan's development is concerned, Richard opines that he is doing as well or better than any of the playgroup kids.

Upon our return from the playground, I find that I've been given the assignment of cooking the chicken, Shirley and Jill having decided through some atavistic reasoning process that the male host should be allotted that privilege. I'm not long on the job, however, before certain parties think I need supervision. "Craig, you're going to burn that meat if you don't take it off the fire soon!" Jill yells down from the kitchen window, apparently noticing how, being heavily involved in conversation, I've neglected my chef duties.

"O.K., O.K., Julia Child, you come down here and stand in the inferno for a while. Shirley and I can continue our conversation in the house while you get the opportunity to do things right down here," I reply. I gesture to Shirley to join me in cooler circumstances. In the kitchen, we set up the kids' meal at a separate table, and I pump Shirley for her opinions.

"Good grief, Craig, the child's been a perfect angel today. He played by himself at the sandbox and didn't bother anyone. And as far as his development is concerned, he's got a terrific amount of speech, and he knows a lot of simple concepts—I mean what are you looking for?" I sheepishly nod my head and glance over at the table where the kids are going to eat. Jessica has preempted the chairs that were to be for her and Jordan and, in their stead, has placed two of her dolls. She continues with the fantasy by serving an imaginary meal to her friends. As I watch this imaginative play unfold, I realize that this is something Jordan never does. It's just a passing observation; I write it off. Every kid develops at his own pace.

June 27, 1984

Milestones of the week include eating with a fork consistently and by preference, creating this sentence: "Make the sand go off the shovel," and pointing out that there are "two" of an object that he sees. He also puts an "s" on the end of the named object—sometimes inappropriately, as in "two mans."

Clear blue skies and temperatures in the low eighties, a jewel of a July day in Baltimore as my parents arrive for a Sunday afternoon visit. We have so much to catch up on, not having seen each other for a few months. This is the third time I've seen my father over the eleven-month period since his surgery, and on each occasion he has looked a little better to me. Today he has an uncharacteristic smile on his face and an almost jauntiness to his step as he walks over from the car to greet us. As we talk, I notice another thing about him. His speech is almost as clear as it was before the operation. I am now certain that he is over the hump.

When they arrive, Jordan is out back playing in his sandbox, and, as always, I'm anxious to have Mom and Dad see him. I suggest a long walk—the mile and a half route that defines the perimeter of our development—to show off their grandson's stamina and the block of new custom-built houses we call "millionaire's lane." Dad opts for lounging with the Sunday paper, but the rest of us head on down the access road that leads away from our property.

Even though this path is fairly steep, Jordan pushes ahead of the pack. "What do you think, Mom?" I say pointing out Jordan's snappy pace. "Is he Baby Olympics material, or what?" Mom slowly breaks into a tolerant and knowing smile suggestive of her forgiveness of a son now become an over-proud father. But that same smile reveals her own happiness at seeing this felicitous grandchild bounding ahead, white locks trailing in the sun.

After our whirlwind tour of the neighborhood, we settle down on the porch for visiting. We get our usual extensive medical report as well as briefings on the doings of my two brothers. Aside from the typical concerns over my older brother's marital and financial status, most of the news is good. For our part, the briefing focuses on all of the new tricks that Jordan can do as well as the obligatory showing of the garden. Because Mom and Dad are only spending the day, we decide to have an early dinner followed by a third, and two-month-delayed, birthday party for Jordan.

Indulgent parents that we are, we provide a third cake adorned with appropriate accoutrements, and Jordan, to everyone's amusement, takes up singing on his own behalf. Along with other gifts, a Fisher Price farm set is presented to the birthday boy. But, to our dismay, Jordan has a very negative reaction to our suggestions that he play with it. His behavior, in fact, is sufficiently out of proportion with the situation that Jill and I are a little embarrassed. Mom dismisses the incident as so much terrible twoness, but I notice a different expression on her face as they leave for home that evening. It is an expression that betrays an awareness of some unforseen danger; not unlike the way I imagine an animal might look when it senses an impending earthquake.

During this third summer I spend with Jordan, the isolated incidents of negativism, quirky language, resistance to change, cognitive stagnation, and the desire to be alone begin to form a pattern. At times, he will "play" by himself for periods of up to an hour, all the while repeating phrases he frequently uses or has heard in books. He expresses little or no interest in other children, and he shows very little propensity for imaginative play. The curiosity he exhibited in the previous summer seems to have totally disappeared, and he is no longer consistently of good mood. Jill and I occasionally discuss these matters, but without urgency. We have plausible explanations for all of the things that concern us. If he isn't developing as rapidly in the cognitive domain as he had done in the past, well then he is concentrating on his physical skills. After all, he is climbing on everything and kicking balls and running like a kid much older than he. If he likes to play by himself, what difference does that make? "That's exactly the way I was as a kid," Jill remembers. And if he isn't uniformly pleasant anymore, then maybe he's just being a typical two year old. What could possibly be wrong with him?

In pursuit of confirmation of our own comfortable theories, we solicit the opinions of friends and relatives. It seems each has a similar story of developmental gaps, of unusual behavior, of inflexibility or of other problems among their own children. The message is clear, "Not to worry!" So, for the most part, we don't.

Jill records these observations of Jordan at 26 months:

August 18, 1984

After a Saturday night crab feast at my parents' house, we left Jordan there and are going to the Poconos

*Sunday A.M. Jordan was very aware that he was being
left; cried "want to go home" and "go see Mommy."
We'll be gone till Tuesday, and it was hard to leave him.*

   *He is not really patient about being read to these
days, but he will sit by himself and look through several
books. He runs through most pages quickly, but stops to
recite the text of a random page. His most frequent requests are for juice and "Mommy lie down on your
blanket," meaning that he and I will spread his blanket on
the living room floor and lie on it. Then we look at each
other and say, "Mommy lying down, and Jordan lying
down."*

   *Earlier this week we took Jordan to Berkeley Springs
(the site of my parents' summer cottage), and he loved
swimming in the "pool" and playing in the sand. He tod-
dled out into the neck-high water and would have kept
right on going unchecked. We also took him to the county
fair, where he rode on a train and the merry-go-round,
and cried coming off.*

   *Jordan makes funny sentences such as "Put it back
on again the shoe."*

As summer comes to an end, Jill and I decide that we
should get away from Jordan for a few days. Not since he was
born have we spent so much as a night without him; and we
have been thinking out loud of late that we may be simply too
involved with him and that our constant, and perhaps over-
bearing, attention might be contributing to his shyness. Besides, we haven't had any kind of vacation at all in four years,
so we feel we've earned one.

   Jill books us a very nice room in a nearby mountain resort
for a song. The weatherman cooperates with three gloriously
sunny and cool days, and we have a terrific time swimming,
hiking, overeating, and almost totally forgetting about Jordan.
Actually, he remains uppermost in our individual thoughts,
but a pre-agreed upon moratorium on conversation about him

is strictly upheld. On the afternoon we are to leave, the resort holds an outdoor banquet with live entertainment—a soft, folksy guitar player whose pleasant voice sweetly fills the mini valley in front of the hotel.

These last few days of outdoor activity have added a deeper tone to the wonderful brownness of Jill's summer skin—an effect which compliments those light blue eyes, diaphanous to her soul. Noticing this as we stand in the buffet line, I run my hand the length of her arm as if to confirm her reality. The warmth of it passes through my arm and enters the interior of my being. Almost involuntarily my eyes turn upward to the smiling blue abyss above.

At dusk that evening we pull into the Kaberles' driveway. My mother-in-law is out to greet us before we are out of the car. In a weary voice she details the events of Jordan's life over the past three days, which include a bout with the flu and nights of broken sleep. She is glad we're home for more reasons than one. Everyone wants to start fresh on the morrow, so we pack up the toddler gear and make ready for the trip home.

Carol issues the usual disclaimer about how Jordan was no trouble at all as we thank her and Kabe profusely for the babysitting service. In her eyes is the same unspoken look of concern that I noticed from my own mother a month earlier. Perhaps this extended period of dealing with Jordan has led her to some ineffable realizations about the path he is headed on. At any rate, whatever thoughts she has about the matter stay with her—until the dam breaks loose.

Even as the evidence accumulates that something is wrong with Jordan, no one articulates it. He is such a different child that no one quite knows how to put his finger on just what the problem might be. In isolation, all of his oddities are things we have seen in other children his age. Moreover, for each thing about him that disturbs us, there seems to be something we can try to do to remedy the problem. Thus, for example, his shyness might be abated by increased contact with other children; or his language peculiarities might be remediated through requiring him to say things correctly. Most importantly, however, no one diagnoses the situation as a serious problem because the way he is doesn't fit into any "disorder schemata" available to us. He clearly isn't mentally retarded, for no retarded two-year-old knows or can do as much as he. He isn't insane, for though he is peculiar, his eccentricities don't amount to psychosis. And, from our limited frame of reference, he isn't even autistic, because he has always been affectionate. In the absence of a label, we think of him as immature, and genuinely believe that he's just going through a phase. ❄

❄

❄

❄

❄ I once read that October is the month in which the body produces the most endorphins—those chemicals that create the natural high. Today is one of those days which seems to confirm that notion. In the air about is that perfect combination of wind and sun that makes the task of putting the garden to sleep for the winter more a joy than a chore. There is beside me a beautiful child pushing his toy shovel into the soft earth. On the deck my good friend is fooling around with one of her flower boxes. And all around I am in the midst of fields and forces that silently work to insure that the center holds. Peace and a sense of well-being appear almost to be imposed on me. I think of the line from the

Twenty-third Psalm: "He maketh me to lie down in green pas-
tures. . . He restoreth my soul." And, indeed, He increaseth
my production of endorphins.

My gardening work is finished now: the earth is turned
over, and it's not quite two o'clock. "Come on, Jord. Let's go
to the playground. You can ride on the blue plane," I suggest,
realizing that I haven't paid much attention to him all day. In
a couple of hours my brother-in-law and his wife will be coming over for dinner, so this is my last shot at play time for the
day.

"Go to playground," he answers back quickly, while abandoning his shovel to race up to the house. Smiling, I pick up
his tool and follow him up the hill. It's just a half-mile walk to
the playground, but I'm beat from the gardening so I recom-
mend that we take the car. This idea apparently meets with
Jordan's approval, as he loudly repeats, "Go in the brown car!"

In a minute, we're there, and the little guy appears
ecstatic as he opens the gate to enter the yard. He heads
straight for the sliding board, which has recently become a
favorite, while I perch on a nearby platform. Jordan has become so sure of foot going up ladders that I've stopped spot-
ting him and can now enjoy watching him from a distance.
After a couple of trips down, he is no longer getting a swift
ride, for the mud which has gotten on his pants at the end of
each slide has accumulated, making the sliding a slow business. Noticing his problem, I suggest that he play on another
piece of equipment. To my dismay, the suggestion produces a
huge protest. I try pointing out that he has mud on his pants,
but he will have nothing of the explanation. When the
protest escalates into a full-blown temper tantrum, I reach for
his hand to pull him away from the slide. But before I can
touch him, he moves away and does something which startles
me; he begins to whirl around and make a whistling sound. It

looks so bizarre that I back off immediately and tell him he can slide down one more time, and then we'll go. It takes him a few moments to finally settle down, and, when he does, he doesn't go back to the slide but, instead, heads for the car.

"Just because you've spent most of your adult life working with young children and have never seen this kind of behavior doesn't mean that you panic," I think almost out loud as I follow Jordan back to the car. I'm shaken by this episode, but for a while longer at least I'll continue to take my vision from the heart.

When Jordan and I return home, Jill is in the front yard finishing up some raking with an entourage of what are undoubtedly unsolicited helpers. The three neighborhood children have apparently convinced her that she would be much happier doing her job if, with their help, it took twice as long. Seeing this ready-made opportunity for Jordan to have some peer interaction, Jill and I work together to make a big pile of leaves for the kids to play in. The two older children take to this activity right away, taking turns covering and uncovering each other. Jordan and the other two-year-old hang back a minute to survey the goings-on. They both eventually react to the situation, and in their different reactions they tell a story whose moral we will be only another six weeks in learning. The little girl, seeing that her siblings are enjoying themselves immensely, ultimately joins them in the game to complete a boisterous trio. Jordan, on the other hand, acts totally uninterested in the scene and walks toward the backyard. Even when Jill and I shrilly exhort him to play, he remains unmoved, looking away into the distance.

Jill's final entry before we receive Jordan's diagnosis shows how our concerns have grown:

October 9, 1984

Just as Craig and I go through cycles of mood, Jordan seems to have periods of high and low, usually lasting one to three weeks. The lows are thankfully shorter than the highs, but they seem interminable when we are in their midst.

Our biggest concern about Jordan at this point is his shyness. He dislikes going into strange houses, instantly putting one thumb in his mouth and the other on his earlobe, and clinging to Craig or me. Last Saturday at Doug and Jennifer's, he wouldn't play in their children's rooms unless I was in there with him. The shyness extends to every household except Marietta's.

He also raised Cain when we recently left him with Aunt Kathy, whom he really loves. We are dealing with it by trying to take him to people's houses as much as possible and by assuming he'll outgrow it.

Jordan's speech is still developing, but more slowly. He has learned the vital use of "no,"—generally, it comes out as "no, no, no" when an unwelcome suggestion or command is made.

He goes to bed very easily and quietly at 9:00-9:30. We go into his room, get into his bed and lie with him, usually telling him a story or reviewing the day's activities. Then we sing him a song, kiss him, and leave. Jordan often stays awake for another hour, talking to himself, but almost never crying for company. He has been out of the crib since Labor Day—a move which he did not appear to even notice.

Unfortunately, the next step—out of diapers—seems a long way off. Jordan is quick to change the subject whenever it comes up.

II

*I*t is an artificial division, to be sure, in that Jordan was unquestionably born with a brain disorder resulting in a condition we at present call autism, but after we finally realize
that something is seriously wrong with him, and that that
something has a name, a symptomatology, a prognosis, I am
unable to conceive of his life as having anything less than two
parts. What gives rise to this belief that, although the seeds of
his autism may have been present from birth, his early
development was not a seamless web? It is the obvious fact
that, at one point in his life, Jordan learned, displayed affection, enjoyed social interaction, and had a positive disposition. By twenty months of age all of these attributes were less
in evidence, and by three and a half they were virtually gone.
Additionally, his life derives some of its "before and after"
quality from the fact that there exists a specific moment in
time when we go from seeing Jordan as a peculiar but normal
child to realizing that his peculiarities threaten his very
humanity.

Knowing that moment in time when Jordan, in our
minds, enters another dimension, enables us to put parameters
around that first part of his life. It is as if he has died from one
existence and returned in another form. His first life is short,
lasting two years, seven months, and thirteen days. It is like
some beautiful annual whose seeds God has misplaced, blos-
soming its brief season and then vanishing forever; though,
even now, its memory can emit a radiance that is startlingly
fresh. As I walk through his time with you, we are at the
threshold of Jordan's second life, and I am half tempted to
issue the warning that appeared at the entrance to hell in

Dante's *Divine Comedy:* "Abandon all hope, ye who enter here."

It is Thanksgiving, ironically my favorite holiday of the year, and all of the Kaberle family are together for the traditional holiday meal. Our patriarch is undertaking that ritual for which he is consistently and mercilessly taunted—the family photo. Having two more of us to get into the picture this year, he is able, only after considerable time and effort, to obtain the proper angle for the shot. Then, after setting the timer, he races off to get into the picture himself. Of course, the operation fails a couple of times, and, by the time he gets it right, we're all a little less smiley, especially Jordan, who is hungry. But it isn't long before the clanging of silverware and the ebb and flow of laughter are filling the evening as completely as Carol's delicious dinner is filling our stomachs. It must seem a wonderful time for my in-laws, surrounded as they are by their happy, healthy and successful children, as well as two grandchildren; enjoying good health themselves; and anticipating the prospect of a full and active retirement.

Incredibly, in less than two weeks, it will all explode in their faces.

During the week after Thanksgiving, Jill learns that our friend Sue (the widow of the friend who died suddenly earlier in the year) has moved to a house not far from ours. She calls Sue and sets up a dinner engagement for the upcoming Sunday. It doesn't promise to be a light and easy evening, as Chris's absence will be unsettling, but Sue is a resilient character and has already gotten far along on the task of putting her life back together. Besides, her two boys should be ideal playmates for Jordan.

Being December, it's already dark when Sue and her boys arrive, so I suggest that I play with the children in the basement while Sue and Jill put dinner together and catch up on each other's lives. I'm happy with this arrangement in that I'll get a chance to see how the kids react to each other in the absence of their mothers. It turns out that my worst suspicions are confirmed. Not only are Sue's boys interactive with each other, but they are also eager to enlist me and Jordan in their play. Contrarily, Jordan simply ignores their overtures, eschewing their company for the seemingly mindless activity of pushing his school bus around the perimeter of the room.

The younger of Sue's boys, who is actually six months younger than Jordan, makes several attempts at getting Jordan to use his vehicle more imaginatively, all of which are summarily disregarded. After a short while, Jordan's would-be playmate abandons his efforts and joins his brother and me in a game of catch. As I play with the two kids willing to play, I notice something else, and my failure to have observed it before now seems mindboggling. It is this: Jordan, unlike the other little two-year-old, has no ability or desire to hold a conversation. This observation is made more incredible by the realization that Jordan probably has twice the vocabulary of his friend.

The rest of the evening goes horribly as Jordan clings to Jill and, in other ways, manifests his immense deficits in the "skill" of being human. When the visit is over, there is stunned apprehension. Like a slap in the face from some Zen master, this experience jolts us into a reality which we neither can nor want to comprehend. Yet, its sudden presence is so definitive that we can no longer turn away.

How macabrely ironic it all seems! Here we have this friend who witnesses such personal tragedy—the death of her husband—to usher in the marked year of 1984, and now, unwittingly, she is present at the beginning of our own tale of woe as the year comes to a close. It certainly gives credence to the philosopher Arthur Schopenhauer's notion that when we

look back on life its events will often have the quality of seeming to have been written. But how do we make sense of such
an author whose intricate plots and inscrutable purpose appear so beyond us?

In the week that follows our revelation, we hardly know
how to proceed. We are aware that Jordan's problem requires
immediate attention and are thus grateful when we remember
that he is scheduled to see the pediatrician in less than ten
days. Prior to the visit Jill calls to alert him to our concerns, in
order that he might evaluate Jordan from the standpoint of his
development. We also strategize as to other actions we might
consider. We both feel that his presence at the baby sitter's
(though we are happy with her) might be causing him to be
anxious or immature, so Jill decides to explore the possibility
of going half time at work. Additionally, we think of ways to
involve Jordan with other children. Along with having him
spend more time with the neighbor's kids, we agree to make
"Sunday school" at the Kaberles' church a regular thing.

Of course, we immediately relate our concerns to my in-
laws, who are, as they have always been, there when we need
them. In the middle of the week Carol calls to invite us to
spend all day on Sunday at their place. She suggests that in
the morning Jordan can go with her to Sunday school, and
then later on we can have dinner by the fireplace and try to
sort things out.

When Sunday morning arrives, they are waiting for us at
the door, all reassuring smiles. Only ninety minutes later,
when they return from church, the smiles are gone. Today is
their day of reckoning. Apparently, the fears Carol has been
harboring for some time are crystallized in the experience of
Sunday school.

Sensing that I'm not ready for this encounter, I quickly
take Jordan out to the back yard, while Jill and her mother

confer in the kitchen. Some time later, Jill comes out to the back yard to inform me that she and her dad are taking Jordan to the playground. She says nothing of her conversation with her mother, but simply indicates that there's a plate of food waiting for me inside. When I get into the kitchen, I find I've no appetite. I won't be able to eat until I've spoken to Carol. I hear her loading the washer in the utility room, so I pull myself out of the chair and go down to confront her.

In the twelve years that I've known her, I have never seen Carol just staring into space, yet as I enter the doorway to the utility room, that appears to be what she is doing. Her back is toward me as I start to speak. "We have a problem, don't we Carol." The words sound so faint that I wonder if they reach her.

But she turns to show her flushed face and blurts out in a voice that is at once a scream and a whimper, "Oh, Craig, he's so different; so different from the other children!"

Her body is shaking, and this outpouring of desperation from a woman I love drains from me everything that I've kept inside for a week. It's the beginning of the crying time.

Around the fireplace that evening we are the congregation of the befuddled. No one has the slightest idea of how Jordan got from Point A to this horrifying Point B, and we're still not sure what to call Point B. Even now, after we've had a day-long venting of our emotions and are beginning to think more rationally, we are unable to make any sense of it. It is clear that Jordan has some kind of syndrome or condition, but what?

Finding this situation almost unbearable, I ask my in-laws if they would take Jill and Jordan home while I go to a nearby college library to do some "research." It's near closing time, but at least I'll have an hour and a half to look for clues. While driving, I formulate a game plan which calls for me to start with the psychology texts and, specifically, to review the references to autism. Having read Bruno Bettelheim's *The Empty Fortress* some years back, I vaguely recall the descriptions of his clients, and think that the similarities between those folks and Jordan might make autism a good starting place.

I have only to open a single book to know that, at the very least, Jordan is autistic-like, and that, more probably, he has full-blown autism. Three typical symptoms give it away: the tendency to repeat phrases, the absence of the words "yes" and "I" from the vocabulary, and the propensity to self-stimulate (of late Jordan has been throwing his fingers in front of his face).

The diagnosis seems easy, but then comes the hard part, the prognosis. Almost every source I examine talks about a 75 to 90 percent probability of mental retardation. And the statistics on institutionalization are equally grim. Moreover, there is very little in the literature which would come under the heading of "promising practices."

I can't bring myself to believe that it's that final, yet, as soon as I'm sure that this is the answer, I go to the phone and call Jill. My words hit the receiver like a dead basketball against asphalt, "It's autism, Jill."

"Oh, Christ, Craig! You're in the library less than an hour and already you have him diagnosed," she shoots back defiantly.

"Well, I think you'll see what I mean when I tell you more about it later." There is a period of silence which lets me know that, as far as she is concerned, the conversation is over, so I gently lay down the receiver and head for home.

When we visit the pediatrician later that week, there are no revelations or surprises. During the examination, he attempts to get Jordan to write with a pencil and to perform a few other tasks— each without much success. He also does some cursory tests for soft signs of neurological problems. And he asks us a number of questions about Jordan's behavior. In the end, he agrees that there is a problem but shies away from a specific diagnosis. He recommends neurological testing and offers to expedite the matter by making the initial contact.

It is reassuring to know that, chances are, Jordan doesn't have some readily identifiable brain disorder, but we are still left with the empty feeling of not being sure of what we're fighting. Things will happen quickly enough, though. By the next day we are scheduled for a consultation with a neurologist at Baltimore's Kennedy-Krieger Institute. And the following week Jordan will have both psychological and neurological evaluations. The jury will be in before the start of the new year. ❄

❄

❄

❄

❄ I said earlier that the human spirit has an uncanny ability to find beauty in the most unyielding of circumstances. Now it seems I must retract, for, in this December season of scurrying preparation for the upcoming Christmas celebration, we are left stranded at the North Pole, frozen in an eternal Arctic night of unremitting cold. Our icy exteriors are laid bare for the rest of the world to see, and thus we pile guilt on top of grief for having to be the harbingers of bad tidings in the "season of light."

The first in what will eventually seem a lifetime of evaluations of Jordan is the psychological assessment. Essentially an I.Q. test, this developmental battery reveals that Jordan is functioning in the low normal range. The administering

psychologist, seemingly sensing our dismay, is quick to offer
disclaimers regarding the predictive ability of such assessments
with children Jordan's age. She also points out his unusual
background and the possibility that he didn't cooperate fully
with the process. The explanations aren't of much help,
though. Seventy-one doesn't sound like a very happy number
when you're talking about your child's IQ.

In the car we have our moment of silence or, more accurately, speechless incredulity. By what convoluted process of
reverse development did this child of apparent promise plum-
met down the chute to near mental retardation? And, if his
drop from bright to dull normal occurs in ten months, where
will it end? Then too, what kind of mechanism is at work
here? One that doesn't affect physical development, or the
early acquisition of language and concepts, that's obvious.
Rather, it seems to work its insidious black magic through an
increasing self-isolation, which, because we become intelligent or dull to a large extent as a result of experiences with
others, shuts down the operation of development. It is difficult
to describe the feelings of hopelessness and resentment that
surround us as we travel through the dingy streets of Baltimore
on this gloomy afternoon of truth telling. We pass rows of
dilapidated buildings and scores of people trapped in grinding
poverty and ignorance. We are showered with images from
billboards and store fronts depicting worlds that do not exist.
And we are crushed in an embrace of cognitive dissonance
that holds both the beauty of our little child's face and the
nightmare of his prognosis.

About an hour of daylight is left when Jill and I arrive
home from the evaluation. Sensing that I'm desperate for
some relief, Jill suggests that I get a run in before dinner. I
make the short drive to the local track and set myself in motion. Two or three times during the four-mile run, I am chok-

ing back tears, an experience that has become part of the daily routine for the past two weeks. As I finish the sprint that I make of the last quarter mile, I see the blood-red sun breaking the plane of the horizon, leaving the western half of the sky streaked in orange, red, and pink. It is a holy image, so striking that I feel compelled to stare at it as I catch my breath while sitting on the grass at the edge of the track. I know then that I'm gasping for spiritual oxygen, and I look to this beautiful ball of energy to serve as my intermediary to the force that passes all understanding. I am praying—for what I do not know. I think of a remark that one of the cerebral degenerative patients at a hospital where I once worked used to make: "I'm entitled to something—but I don't know what it is."

I've been sitting too long on the cold ground, and by the time I come out of my trance, the sun has turned away, drawing up its paints and leaving a blackening canvas in its stead. Soaked from the run and chilled to the bone, I step quickly to the car and wend my way through the brightly decorated suburban streets, poised for the birth of Christ.

When I get home, a load of laundry is just finishing up in the dryer, so I decide to postpone my shower until I've put the clothes away. Folding them in our bedroom, I hear Jill trying to involve Jordan in some dinner-related task. It makes me think of how much I admire her as a mother, and I start to cry—no sob—big heaving sobs with large tear drops. Jill must hear this from the kitchen and she is soon in the bedroom confronting me. "You have to stop this constant crying, Craig. It's not doing anybody any good," she says in a calm voice that does not carry the anger I had expected. I wipe my face with my shirt and nod, the blows of December having reduced my ability to respond in these situations to simple gestures.

It is now only a few days before Christmas and, thankfully, I'm off work for a couple of weeks. Working with young children as I do, there has been a bit of a professional dilemma for me these past three weeks. More than any other time of year, Christmas is a time when you can use the joy and anticipation of the children as a vehicle for learning. It only works, though, if you can ride the same wavelength. Scrooge does not teach grade school. I'm hoping too, that the break will give me a little time to start to get some perspective on what is happening in my life. Regardless of what happens to Jordan, everyone in this group is still going to have to help each other out. Our day to day responsibilities in life aren't going to go away.

Thinking along these lines, I decide to make my first act of rehabilitation the creation of an inspirational Christmas card for Jill. Though I have always written her a personalized card for the holidays, inspiration is not my forte, and it takes a long time before I can think of something in the Christmas story which will apply to our current situation. On a tiny piece of red construction paper, I write the following message:

"This year I dreamed of our Christmas including a third spirit: one that would be full of the 'little one's' anticipation and excitement. Nothing could have broken my heart more than the realization that this year would not include that spirit and the fear that it might not for a long while.

"But Christmas has a way of believing in itself, of making us seek the star even when the journey looks long. Like the wise men of old, we have a child to find. How about us packing the camels, crossing the desert, and bringing him back alive."

Things hold up well through Christmas Eve, but in visiting with our extended families between Christmas and New Year's we get a little unglued. In particular, seeing the children of our siblings creates in Jill and me a sense of isolation almost as visible as Jordan's self-imposed separation.

Moreover, we compound the bad form of hurting during the "season to be jolly" with an inability to explain to our relatives just what has happened to Jordan.

The coup de grace is delivered on the 27th, the day of Jordan's neurological evaluation. We return to the scene of earlier crimes, the Kennedy-Krieger Institute, where we enter the lobby with the trepidation of children sneaking into an abandoned house rumored to be haunted. And like such children, it's not long before we've convinced ourselves that we've come upon a truly spooky place. Once inside, we are directed to take a seat in a waiting area which is actually just an extension of the lobby. It turns out to be an apt appellation, this "waiting area," for here we will wait for about forty-five minutes before we see the neurologist. And during that wait a pageant of the doomed passes before us: children in helmets, children with involuntary motor movements, children with faraway looks which seem to emanate from distances too great to be reached through human effort. After a while, I stop looking in the direction of the entrance and try, instead, to concentrate on Jordan. Perhaps he has a sense of where he is, for today he is unhappier than I have seen him in a long time. He is also acting weirder, doing a lot of self-stimulatory stuff, like spinning and making a low whistling sound.

Finally, the neurologist arrives, and the evaluation can begin. It looks, from a layman's point of view, to be a glorified rerun of what the pediatrician and the psychologist did. There are some attempts to get Jordan to perform tasks; there is an examination of how he interacts with social toys; there is the search for soft signs of neurological malfunction; and there is an inspection of his gait. Since nothing immediate hits the eye, there will be blood tests and, of course, an EEG.

When it's over, we don't know much more than we did before, except that the doctor is certain that there is developmental delay and that Jordan will require special education. But lingering questions remain for which we are hopeful of a response. First, since we had supplied him with our diary at the initial consultation, we wonder if the doctor has any thoughts on how it could be that Jordan developed so well for the first two years of his life and then declined so precipitously. From his reaction I get the impression that he has not considered the document as particularly germane to his diagnosis—though he does mention that he thought it was "beautiful." In fact, I get the distinct feeling that he has dismissed much of what we have said to him about Jordan's early development as so much fond remembrance of a nonexistent past. Second, we question him about what steps we need to take to help Jordan. He has, of course, given this question some prior thought, but he doesn't have specific recommendations beyond placing Jordan in public school special education. And third, we want to know if he thinks the diagnosis is autism. He makes it clear that, as far as he is concerned, it doesn't matter how we label Jordan's problem at this point. It is, instead, more important that we take quick action to make sure that Jordan is receiving an education appropriate for his needs.

After Jordan has had his blood drawn, Jill remains with the doctor to iron out some details about what needs to be done next, so I return with him to the waiting area. By this time, Jordan has had about as much of this place as he would care to tell. He actually bolts for the exit once out in the lobby and, in the process, crashes into the scruffy little Christmas tree that stands pitifully next to the door. In so doing, he knocks two balls off the tree, and they shatter on the floor directly in front of the doorway. He then, inexplicably, throws himself down into the pile of debris and starts crying loudly and inconsolably, while people entering the building pass gingerly around to avoid stepping on us.

It isn't until we're back in the car that he finally settles down. A massive heartache has metastasized to my muscles and head, and the very act of starting the car and driving away seems impossible. Jill has maintained greater strength and is more than a little embittered by my lack of faith. Not sharing my genetic predisposition toward depressive states, she interprets my behavior as representing a permanent tossing in of the towel, and she's determined to nip my defeatism in the bud.

Toward that end, she immediately contacts her parents upon arriving home and notifies them of my insufferable mentality. As they had been several times before, and would be again many times later in that hellish winter, my in-laws are at our door before we are finished with lunch. And my father-in-law launches into me immediately. He is a man who knows the value of not giving up, having seen his young wife almost die of tuberculosis thirty-five years before. His words and demeanor make it apparent that he won't tolerate my behavior, and, as he speaks, I realize that I respect him as much as a person respects his own father. I realize too that what he is saying is true, though it will take some time before I am able to shake my lugubrious attitude.

The first step out of this depressed state for me, as it probably is for many people who have experienced depression brought on by a traumatic event, is taking action. Indeed, both Jill and I become involved in a flurry of activity related to Jordan's condition soon after this low point. We cast a wide net in hopes of finding anything which will be helpful in working with Jordan. We talk to friends, telephone local specialists in autism, and read everything we can get our hands on. Additionally, we make games and puzzles, purchase toys, and come up with strategies for trying to reach him at home.

Our search of the literature suggests that the best results being obtained with autistic kids are occurring in settings where behavior modification techniques are being employed. Most notably, California psychologist Ivar Lovaas has reported considerable success in improving the cognitive and social functioning of autistic children utilizing an intense one-on-one program of instruction grounded in behavior modification techniques—that is, by systematically using rewards and punishment to increase desired behavior and reduce unwanted behavior. The theory behind this approach seems to be that children with autism require a specialized learning environment to shape and improve their ability to attend, especially to social cues such as facial expressions and tone of voice. Ordinarily, these children are greatly at risk of misinterpreting or failing to attend to these cues at all.

Having had some experience in designing such programs for kids with behavior problems, I could attest to their effectiveness in some settings, so decide to undertake the development of a similar program for Jordan. It seems to me that the curriculum should consist of those skills in which the developmental tests have shown Jordan to be deficient, so I gather materials which will help me teach such things as classification, prepositional phrases, putting objects in sequence from shortest to tallest and the like, and the general expansion of his vocabulary. The reinforcers will be the time-honored, and Jordan-appropriate, snacking foods, including peanuts, crackers, and the ubiquitous M&M.

Jordan has been so negative and seemingly out of it lately that I don't enter the project with staunch hopes. But, to my amazement, he takes to the whole thing with incredible enthusiasm. From the second week in January until the middle of February, at least twice a day we enter our special world of the "secret room," the little room adjacent to Jordan's where we hold our daily sessions and where we hope to begin to draw him out of his self-imposed isolation through revival of his interest in learning. The results of this initial effort seem too good to be true. Not only does he appear to enjoy the undertaking, he also begins to learn things at a pace that rivals that of his first twenty months.

Jill can hardly control her enthusiasm in this journal entry from that period:

> *January 29, 1985*
>
> *Amazing progress to report in the last two weeks. Craig and Jordan began working in the "secret room," and Jordan now sits at his table for up to an hour (getting up occasionally) and does insert and formboard puzzles, builds towers, makes trains with blocks, and places objects in various positions in relationship to another object while using the correct preposition to describe the position. He has also learned 13 lower case letters and can now categorize beads according to shape or color. Food rewards did the trick! Now, he'll go in there and work with me, too, though not as long.*
>
> *J is much more responsive and alert now. He is happier and enjoys sustained eye contact. He has rediscovered that he likes being read to and sung to, although he still refuses to sing himself. He is learning to generalize with speech and uses it appropriately to describe pictures he has never seen before. For example, yesterday he described a new picture (in response to "What is the boy doing?" he answered "sweeping the floor with the broom.") He no longer refuses to say bye-bye, and says it, upon being prompted, along with the name of the person who is leaving. He's even beginning to say "hi" with prompting.*

During this four-week period, other hopeful signs emerge. A friend of a friend puts us in touch with a renowned expert in autism. This expert, as well as his daughter-in-law, herself a psychologist, spend several reassuring hours on the phone with us, explaining what is known about autism and how the prognosis for children like Jordan, who receive special education early on, is getting better.

We also come to appreciate that the gloomy reports from the developmental assessments of Jordan may not be as reliable as we once thought. Less than a month after the testing done at the Kennedy Institute, Jordan is given many similar tests as part of an intake evaluation for the school system where he will be a student. Results show widely divergent scores, many of which indicate declines in skills of up to six months. Thus, a language test which was administered in December revealed a 25.5-month level of development, while a similar language test produced a 20-month score when administered in January. The fact that these "on paper" declines show up at a time when he actually seems to be improving, causes us to question the whole assessment process.

Add to all of this the fact that every knowledgeable medical and educational consultant with whom we talk consistently points to Jordan's apparent high level of functioning (for a young child with autism) as a reliable indicator of a good prognosis, and we feel a renewed strength. Once again, we begin to talk confidently of Jordan's future. I even go so far as to suggest that Jordan's rapid progress in our secret room sessions is a sure sign that he will be essentially "normalized" by the time he is seven. ❄

❄

❄

❄

＊ It is late at night in the dead of winter. Outside a frigid wind is blowing a few snow squalls up against our window. Jill emerges quietly from Jordan's room, squinting up at the hall light, and tiptoes into our bedroom. "Why didn't you come and wake me up?" she questions testily as she climbs into bed.

"I was afraid Jordan was still awake. Besides, I got involved in this article. It's about this kid with autism who began to make dramatic improvements in sociability and language after his father had designed and made some special toys for him. Are you interested in reading it?" I ask as I hand the article over to her.

"Not right now, I want to finish *The Siege*," she wearily replies, as she slips under the cover and turns on the light beside her side of the bed. I gather up the several articles that are strewn over the bed and floor and make a sloppy pile of them on top of my bureau.

We have known of Jordan's autism less than two months and already, between us, we have read tens of articles and several books. Some of that reading material has been suggested to us by professionals, some of it we have discovered on our own, and some of it has come to us by way of friends or relatives. Like any reader whose interest is piqued by personal crisis, we tend to be drawn to stories and studies that talk of success. And, in the winter of 1985, there are more than a few "miracle" drugs, methodologies, psychological interventions, and, well, miracles. In this Damascus bazaar of hope can be found stories of autistic-like children who were "cured" or greatly improved by being held firmly for long periods of time, or by being introduced to music, or through the ingestion of any number of dietary supplements or drugs, or by having round-the-clock, one-on-one contact with caring adults or children. We even hear of a case of a twelve-year-old mentally retarded and autistic-like girl whose father discovers, from a chemical analysis of her hair, that she is deficient in some vital nutrient and subsequently enables her to attain normal social and intellectual functioning within months by adding the missing substance to her diet. Holy Laetrile!

When the Sirens sing so sweetly from the shores of hope, it becomes difficult to remain tied to reality's mast. A handful of happy endings tends to drown out the voices of the tens of thousands who have not made it out of autism's black hole. If you were to draw up a probability statement for the situation as it exists today in the United States, for example, you might come up with numbers on the order of, say, 120,000 existing cases, for which a favorable prognosis could not be envisioned for more than 40,000. And this would assume replicability of the best results in education, drug, and psychological treatments. But probability statements are only created by the rational, and, chances are, if you have an autistic child you're not thinking rationally.

When Jordan was making reasonably good progress in our home-designed behavior modification program, we could afford to look at this panoply of hopeful literature as selective shoppers, discarding ideas for lack of scientific rigor or other reasons. Now, however, the first interstadial period is over, and the glaciers are again advancing. Almost as abruptly as Jordan took to the idea of working for food rewards, he now begins to reject it. We try varying the rewards and varying the setting, but it doesn't make a difference. What's more, he begins to close us out in other ways too, by showing less willingness to play, self-stimulating more, and actively avoiding contact with us.

He is also becoming less cooperative with the teacher in his preschool program. This is particularly disheartening, because the first few weeks of Jordan's "formal" education went well. He adjusted pretty easily to the two morning sessions in the developmentally delayed class at the county's special education school and to the teacher's once-a-week visit to our house. For a while he seemed to enjoy the experiences the teacher provided with puppets, paints, and other props aimed at facilitating communication and social skills. But, after a month, he begins to shut out these experiences, too.

This general decline in Jordan's relatedness makes us rethink the way we are trying to help him. Since Jordan has made pretty good progress with speech and cognition over the past month, we decide that maybe we should deemphasize these elements of development temporarily and, instead, concentrate on facilitating sociability. We thus reduce the frequency and length of secret room sessions and take our second step on Jordan's behalf. We decide to get a dog. Again, our search of the literature has indicated that many children with autism respond favorably to pets. Some researchers, who have noticed an increased sociability among autistic children when a pet is introduced, have had particular success in this regard with dogs. It is believed that because dogs are highly social, playful and tolerant, they make excellent playmates for autistic children, who generally have deficiencies in these attributes. With another lead to follow, we are off to the pound.

Wanting to be able to train the dog ourselves, we agree on getting one that isn't too much beyond weaning. We also think that, for Jordan's sake, we should get a dog that won't get too big and that will be reasonably mellow. On that order, we pick up a dog at the local animal shelter that we're told should turn out to be a medium-sized, Lab sort of mongrel that will be an ideal playmate for a small child.

It isn't long before we realize that Jordan doesn't think much of his new friend, Shep, and there's good reason. The dog's constant jumping, nipping, and yipping create a visible anxiety, not only in Jordan, but in everyone else who comes in contact with her. Even several months after the dog has been with us, there is little positive effect on Jordan. In fact, her presence seems to add to the growing tension of the household.

Over the next four months, we try to train Shep to jump, chew, and bark less, but the plan doesn't work. In August she is as hyperactive as when we got her, so sadly we take her back to the animal shelter.

Meanwhile, the second half of winter grinds into spring. Our confidence having been shaken by the apparent failure of two of our efforts, we begin to look like people who need some help again. We are fortunate in that we have a pediatrician who is sensitive to the emotional needs of the parents of his patients. He thinks we would be best served by working with a psychiatrist specially trained to counsel families who are trying to cope with a developmentally delayed child.

Though our own search of the literature has provided little guidance as to where to direct our efforts, we are hopeful that this consultant will come to us with fresh ideas. We begin our sessions with her in March and are immediately heartened by her open and hard-working manner. She is the first physician we've met who appears genuinely interested in Jordan's history and in the line of thinking we are pursuing in working with him. After spending considerable time watching the way we try to teach him, she agrees with our conclusion that Jordan appears capable of learning and interacting appropriately if only he would pay better attention. She is also in agreement with the position we are rapidly forming with respect to how best to get Jordan's attention span to improve; that is, that medical intervention is more likely to succeed than educational intervention.

Along these lines we have been investigating the drug fenfluramine. Neurologist Dr. Edward Ritvo is seeing positive

results for many of the autistic subjects in his initial study at
UCLA. For some, behavioral improvements have been accom-
panied by dramatic gains in IQ; and the best results are being
seen with children who are higher functioning—kids like Jordan. Those experimenting with the drug suggest that it may
work by reducing serotonin levels. Serotonin is a chemical
that helps transmit brain impulses, and studies indicate that
between 30 and 40 percent of autistic people have excessively
high levels of this chemical.

The problem, as we and our psychiatrist see it, is that the
drug is only experimental for this particular application. Its
other legitimate use is as an appetite suppressant. There are
fears that the possible side effects might outweigh potential
benefits. This is the very issue which troubles our pediatrician;
he suggests that we should participate in one of the replication studies which are being planned. But how can we do that
if no nearby city is participating? And, even if we are fortunate enough to have Baltimore or Washington selected as a
site, it will be months before Jordan can actually try the drug.
In a little over a month he will be three, and we are very
aware of the importance of early intervention. Increasingly,
we are impatient with a system that makes it difficult for
patients to try a promising medical treatment.

In an effort to get support for our position we ask the
psychiatrist to work a little on the pediatrician. In what she
thinks will be a part of this process, she gets us an appoint-
ment to discuss fenfluramine and other pharmacological options with a local authority on drug treatments for people with
neurological problems. Surprisingly to us, this doctor is not
particularly enthusiastic about the potential for fenfluramine,
or any other drug currently in use, to significantly help Jordan.
Additionally, he expresses the same concerns as did the
pediatrician about the potential side effects in long-term use,

though he doesn't rule out experimenting with it on a trial basis.

This is not sufficient endorsement for the pediatrician, and so we are back to square one. All the while the debate between the various parties is raging, we are looking around for a way to try the drug if none of our medical team is willing to prescribe it. Our safety valve is an out-of-town doctor friend who has been researching the issue along with us. His position is similar to the pharmacological expert's, and, after weighing the pros and cons, he agrees to prescribe it for us, provided we agree to do some careful monitoring.

Meanwhile, back at the day-to-day ranch, we are failing, as Jill's entry in the diary shows:

April 5, 1985

So many consecutive sad days that I've been unable to write. We live in a cloud, with knots in our throats, and again we cry frequently. Jordan is unhappy, alone, and making no progress. Activity in the secret room is almost nonexistent, attention at home and in school is very poor, and Jordan seems unhappy. He now hates having things done to him—dressing him is a physical battle that leaves me weary and lethargic. Jordan resists any attempts to play with toys, although he has been looking at books alone lately. He wants to be alone; often asks me to leave when we go into his room to read, and increases his self-stimulation (noises and finger wiggling) when we intrude. It appears that he is too confused by the world—cannot sort out various stimuli and cannot make sense of anything.

I feel as though I will never come out of the haze of this life—each day as bad or worse than the day before. Mom and Dad often do better than we do. Mom and Suzy [Jill's sister-in-law] had J. one day this week and he was reported to be much better absent me. Jim was with him yesterday morning and said that J. played very responsively for an hour and a half. But it is simple play—he en-

joys but does not learn. The dog seems to make things
worse by pestering him.

Out back the pale green willow trees are arching their
long arms out like pastel fireworks. They are the first pages in
a spring chapter that will see our woods go from light to forest
green. A year ago at this time, this beautiful vista was a living
metaphor for my life: its sensual bounty a reflection of the dap-
pled tones of my own mental state. Today, though, I live in
T.S. Eliot's April of cruelty. And I am incredulous at the
thought of it being only one April back that these gentle fluctuations of wind, weather, and temperature responsible for all
the flowering and growth seemed so like my own benign shifts
of mood that nurtured the lush emotional landscape growing
within me. So distant it all now seems, for, in my current
chaotic circumstance, I am swinging too violently to even
remember how to respond to the message of Spring.

A major contributor to this feeling of ennui is a growing
kind of "information sickness," brought on by an inundation
of useless data that pours in from seemingly everywhere. By
now, we have the neurologist's report, which describes Jordan
as having a "communication disorder" and being "autistic-
like." And we are generally hearing from other professionals
that Jordan is mildly mentally retarded and probably autistic.
But in this month alone, we will see five different doctors,
each of whom will put his or her own spin on prognosis and
recommendations for action. We will also continue to read
books and dozens of journal, magazine, and newspaper articles.
Moreover, we will get advice from teachers, friends, relatives,
and members of the local chapter of the Autism Society of
America. And through it all, there will only be stagnation.

Gazing down from the deck, as I am on this glorious
spring day, I sense how dizzyingly fast my child is escaping me.
Like a blown-up balloon whose end hasn't been tied, he

dashes back and forth without pause or purpose below me, and this odd behavior is, ironically, symbolic of how quickly his very life seems to be deflating. I, and the others who are trying to reach him, desperately want to catch Jordan before the air runs out, but no one seems to have a clue as to how to do it.

It is now five months since we found out that Jordan has autism, about two months since he has shown any interest in us, and the effects of this experience are beginning to show up in other aspects of our lives. At work I abandon the special projects, such as science fairs, math contests, and pen pal programs that usually make spring a fun time to be involved with children. At home I barely touch the garden that I've always looked forward to. My entire day seems to be a constant struggle to maintain a minimum level of energy—a struggle whose pervasiveness is vividly brought home to me on a bright day in early May.

It is shortly after four when I arrive home from work. I have an hour before I'm scheduled to be at the Kaberles' for dinner; just enough time to get in my daily run. For thirteen years I've been finding the time to run between four and eight miles almost every day. It has been a constant that has kept me in a state of relative equilibrium during some difficult periods, and it has been particularly helpful in fighting off the effects of this terribly stressful time. Once the after-dinner mint in a day rich with experience, now this ritual has become the only staple in my diet of time.

Running has become such a regular part of my life that I hardly take notice of the changes taking place in my body as I run. Except on particularly hot or cold days, there is almost never a struggle. But today is different. About three-quarters of a mile into the run my legs suddenly become remarkably inflexible and heavy, as if I were running in casts. As has been my custom whenever I've felt a little discomfort in the past, I talk myself into continuing for another half mile or so. If I can't straighten things out by then, I figure, I'll stop. This plan, which usually enables me to finish, is of no use at all now. After only another quarter mile, I'm gasping for air, the rest of my body having become as heavy as my legs. I literally don't have the strength to finish five times around the track! Another runner who regularly uses the track at about the same time as I takes enough notice of my unusual behavior to ask if I'm sick. And I'm so dumbfounded by the experience that I wonder whether if, in fact, he's not right.

But, unfortunately, it is not an isolated incident. Over the next two months, I experience this same curious feeling three or four times a week, and I'm never able to get my distance above three miles. And even after I seem to get a hold on the problem, I have occasional lapses into this inexplicable tightening and weakness. Eventually, though, a combination of relaxed breathing and visualizing myself running fluidly before I start each run helps me to overcome the feeling. Later, this small victory over depression would prove to be valuable capital in what will, no doubt, be a life-long process of adjustment.

One of the outcomes of our awful April is our resolve to try fenfluramine. We realize, without our pediatrician having to remind us, that we are playing a form of "Let's Make a Deal," with all sorts of possibilities behind the doors. But if we don't deal, we are left with only the prospect of improvement through education, a prospect for which the pediatrician him-self holds little hope. And, far from making progress, Jordan seems to be standing perfectly still in some respects and regressing in others. Neither the teacher nor the speech therapist who work with Jordan has had special training in working with autistic children, and, though their efforts in trying to reach him are commendable, they appear no better at their task than we. Jordan doesn't seem at all interested in blowing bubbles, or singing, or watching flashing lights, or in any of the activities they try. How long should we hold out hope that they, or we, or he, will somehow miraculously improve? It seems clear: the need for and possibility of improvement using drugs outweighs the potential risks.

Like so many other events which seem poised between revelation and apocalypse, our experience with fenfluramine proves to be far more mundane than we had anticipated. Over a period of about a week, we give him increasing amounts of the drug, culminating in a dosage at the recommended level. There are no noticeable improvements. Although this may not constitute an adequate trial, we decide to dispense with the experiment at least temporarily. Aside from its failure to produce any positive results, the drug appears to make Jordan lethargic. This, and the concern that we are alienating our medical advisors, makes us leery of continuing on our uncertain path.

An experiment with a promising drug, a brief flirtation with behavior modification, the acquisition of a pet, and four months of traditional special education, and we are nowhere. Instinctively, we turn away from the sources of our frustration. We reduce our reading of the professional literature, we cancel the sessions with the psychiatrist, and we talk less with the staff at Jordan's school. Now what we want is some advice from people who have been there—contact with other parents of autistic children. But we don't have a big market to draw from. There is one other autistic child at Jordan's school, and there are several couples whom Jill has met at the autistic society meetings who have children around Jordan's age. During that summer, we begin exchanging visits with a couple of those families, hoping to cultivate relationships that will provide us with support and information. Our first visit with one of those families stands out in my mind.

On a hot day in early summer, we are driving through the neighborhood behind Baltimore's Memorial Stadium. As we stop at a light not far from the centerfield opening of that ballpark, I glance at the rows and rows of empty seats in the upper deck. For thirty years I have been going to baseball games and sitting in such seats. Since I've lived in Maryland, I've spent many a night in that very enclosure, soaking in the greenness of the field and the variegated colors of the sky as the evening drifted into night. Stopped at this light I consider how—had Jordan been normal—it would have probably been only one more summer before I would have been introducing him to baseball, the way my own father had done for me thirty years before. But how could this "boy in a bubble"—imperme-able to the magnetism that draws people together—ever respond to such a social game as baseball? No, even at this early point in his life, it seems certain that there won't be baseball in Jordan's future. Despite the trivial quality of this in-evitable deprivation, the sadness of its realization grips me like a muscle cramp, while silent cheers pour from the stands.

The light changes, and we travel the final two blocks to Theresa and Andor's. At the door of their tiny row house be-hind the stadium the three of them are waiting as we get out of the car. I am immediately struck with the beauty of their child, Darren. About a year older than Jordan, Darren appears to be the classic autistic child. Now he is flapping his hands and jumping; later he will run around the house opening doors and turning off and on lights. He will also show a fas-cination with and facility for using the VCR. And his parents show us his drawings, which seem beyond his years, and far beyond his other abilities.

We are not with this family an hour, and I realize that the time I've spent here has already been immensely more helpful than the five or six hour sessions we had with the psychiatrist. Here, just like us, were people dealing with the day-to-day tribulations of autism. We can relate an experience and know we're being understood. We can joke about Jordan or share our concerns over his future without feeling that we're being pitied. It is a wonderful feeling that we would enjoy several more times before the Skopnes moved to New York.

Another thing that I notice about our day with the Skopnes as we are on our way home is how, for the first time in over six months, I compared my child with another. During his first two and a half years, I was constantly assessing Jordan's development vis-a-vis other children. At playgrounds, in grocery stores, and everywhere else we would encounter kids, I was always sizing Jordan up against his peers. But since we've known about Jordan's autism, it has seemed as if he has no peers, and I have been barely able to look at little children, knowing that in seeing too much of their brightness, I might become absorbed in Jordan's darkness. Today, though, I can look at Jordan next to this child, not so much to determine who is better at what, but to analyze how Jordan is different; perhaps, I think, to get an understanding of what motivates him.

One revelation that comes out of this thought process is a better understanding of the lack of clarity in my sense of autism. Darren is remarkably different from Jordan. He doesn't speak nearly as well, but he has some abilities and the seeds of still others. He is more difficult to manage, but shows far more interest in his surroundings. He functions higher in visual areas, but is less able to communicate. I ruminate at the time that it would be wonderful to be able to create a composite of their attributes. And I come away from this initial experience convinced that autism is the inverse of the Hindu sense of God—not one thing that men call by many names, but many things for which there is but one label.

If my experience with Darren is an awakening of sorts, then my ongoing contacts with Alex are confirmation of that newly derived insight. Alex, also a year older than Jordan, is a student at Jordan's school. Since Alex is the only other child showing similar characteristics to our son's, the school staff have been sort of pointing him out to us from the beginning. Additionally, we have had fleeting contact with him and his parents as fellow participants in a swim period for hand-icapped kids on Saturdays.

After a few such encounters, we learn that Alex has never been diagnosed as autistic. Clearly, however, he exhibits many of the core traits of that disorder. He is, for example, self-stimulatory. He also displays an inflexibility regarding changes in routines, a definite characteristic of autism. And, judging from the reports of his parents, his speech is largely repetitions of phrases out of context. Typical of this behavior is his amus-ing habit of reciting commercials and his penchant for whis-tling the theme song from the quiz show "Jeopardy."

During the summer, there are more opportunities to ob-serve Alex, as he and Jordan are, again, fellow students at the county's summer school for children with disabilities. Since I am, as usual, off for the summer, I make a few appearances at the school, not so much to see the program, which we have in-creasingly written off as inappropriate for Jordan, but rather to see how Jordan reacts to the instruction he is receiving and to the other children. It is in this setting that I learn how dif-ferent the species "autism" is from other members of the genus "handicapped," and how different individual members of the autistic species can be from one another.

I receive my initiation into these mysteries on my first visit to the summer program. Each day, I'm told by the young principal as I enter the building, the children get together for an assembly period. He leads me down the hall to where the assembly is to take place, explaining to me that this is a time when the children sing and view little vignettes put on by members of the staff, volunteers, or fellow students.

Today, as I find my observation post in the assembly area, the children begin the program by singing the song "You Are Special," an upbeat number emphasizing the positive aspects of individuality whatever the source of differences between people. Like episodes from the old T.V. show "Rocky and Bullwinkle," or certain bits done on "Sesame Street," the message of the song, though ostensibly for the benefit of children, appears to be better appreciated by the adults. The kids, nevertheless, perform it with gusto. Here in this enlarged hallway, the beautiful faces of children with Down syndrome, cerebral palsy, and orthopedic conditions surround that of my own little boy. And I can see clearly just how dramatically Jordan and his autistic classmate stand out in the crowd. Whereas the overwhelming majority of the children are earnestly attempting to join in the chorus, despite their disabilities, Jordan maintains a placid indifference to it all. Not far from him is Alex, who is being restrained by an adult, due, no doubt, to a tendency to opt out of such activities with his feet. Like Jordan, Alex is a consummate non-joiner.

Observing Jordan and Alex in this group of children, most of whom appear more impaired than they, I get a sense that, unlike their schoolmates, their primary deficit has less to do with a lower trajectory of learning potential, than with an almost total refractoriness to participation. Thus, if learning results from a combination of motivation, aptitude, and concentration, then the autistic child is differentiated from a child who is simply retarded by having, in at least a significant number of cases, a higher aptitude, better powers of concentration, and considerably poorer motivation.

Following this line of thinking, it is obvious that Jordan has a much higher aptitude for learning language than most of his agemates here, considering that he learned to talk at an age falling within the normal range. One might make a similar case for Darren's visual skills. And all three of the autistic children I know have demonstrated unusual abilities to concentrate, if learning to operate fairly sophisticated machinery, or memorizing a lengthy commercial, or working for an hour learning age-appropriate concepts counts as evidence. But in exhibiting motivation in order to learn and grow and participate, the child with autism is far more disadvantaged.

It is in this area, too, that one can clearly see the differences between the autistic children. Jordan, for example, seems unmotivated to participate in any normal play or learning activities. Alex at least uses his powers of concentration to learn commercials and to attend to the details of his various rituals. And Darren is interested in art and machinery, so long as those activities don't interfere with his powerful compulsions to fixate on lights or doors. I can't help but wonder at this time, "Who has the greatest advantage, the child with the best speech, or the child who manifests the most interest in his environment?" In the summer of 1985, no one can be certain. ❄

⁎ In addition to cultivating our contacts with these families, Jill has been regularly increasing her circle of acquaintances through participation in the local chapter of the Autism Society of America. Not being a joiner by nature, I have shied away from becoming involved in these efforts. But a desire to determine how better to cope with autistic parenthood, and a strong push from Jill to participate, prove sufficient to get me involved.

My first memorable experience with the organization occurs at the annual picnic. It is here that I get a glimpse of the future, and it makes me shudder. In attendance are about ten people with autism; two adults, several adolescents, and a handful of children of elementary school age. Along with parents, various professionals are there too. Jill is most interested in having me meet the son of the president of the organization. He is an adult who has sufficiently overcome his autism to graduate from college and earn an advanced degree in geology. This is an incredible feat, and he turns out to be an interesting fellow, but the difficulties he exhibits in social interaction are ample to serve notice that recovery from something like autism is indeed a life-long process. The other autistic adult at the picnic is unmistakably disabled, though normal in appearance. His conversation consists of denigrating references to obscure rock and roll bands, delivered in a voice almost devoid of inflection. It is not simply difficult to converse with him, it is painful.

But, more painful still is to watch the behavior of the adolescents and their beleaguered parents. A couple of these youngsters are wanderers, and they are particularly adept at avoiding their parents, who spend the bulk of their time at the picnic chasing their offspring around. Other parents, whose children do not endanger themselves or others, have the luxury of standing around making normal conversation. They

don't, however, have the freedom to ignore the bizarre behavior of their kids, though some seem to have become inured
to it.

Many of the parents and professionals that I meet speak of
the problems of appropriate placements for children, or of
trying to implement quality programs with inadequate resour-
ces. And there is universal concern about what happens to
the young adults among this population. None of what I hear
or see at this event measures up to the bright pronouncements
of a better future for people with autism that came so readily
from the "experts" with whom I had earlier spoken. ✱

✱

✱

✱

✱ In this torrid summer of 1985 I am beginning to feel an
affinity for India's Ramanandi, those perpetual Hindu pilgrims
who spend their lives visiting various holy sites. For Jill and I
have traveled many paths on the trail of the antidote for
autism. The most recent shrine we have visited offers hope to
the suppliant whose condition is brought on by metabolic mal-
functioning. In late spring we learn of the work of Dr. Mary
Coleman, a physician treating autistic-like patients through
dietary restrictions and supplements aimed at attaining proper
chemical balance. Some autistic children have been found to
have high levels of purine enzymes in their systems. In others,
low levels of calcium have been observed. In some cases, the
autistic-like patients that Dr. Coleman and others have
treated with dietary adjustments have made behavioral and
cognitive improvements. Since Jordan has long had what we
thought were unnatural cravings for certain kinds of foods

(cheese, bread, barbecue sauce, apple juice), we have believed it possible that his unusual eating patterns might actually represent an effort at self-healing. If this is so, then it seems feasible that this kind of treatment might prove beneficial.

Our pediatrician is aware of the work of Dr. Coleman and agrees that going through her screening process would be a reasonable step for us to take. Before long we have arranged for the workup to be done with a doctor who is collaborating with Dr. Coleman. And, not long after that, we receive the results. That is, the non-results. Another dead end. ❅

❅

❅

❅

❅ It is now a week after we learned that Jordan has no discernible metabolic abnormalities, and he and I are on our mile and a half walk around the neighborhood: the same walk we have been doing almost daily for over a year. It is a sweltering July afternoon, and I question my common sense for undertaking this activity on such a day. But Jordan doesn't seem to mind the heat, and this walk is just about the only thing he really enjoys anymore. Perhaps "enjoys" is too strong a word: let us say that this walk is something he tolerates.

As we move along at a window shopper's pace, I'm struck by how different his whole demeanor has become since we first started doing this a year ago. At that time, he frequently made requests such as asking to be picked up to see signs. He also used to do a little narration as he went along, perhaps referring to passing vehicles or noticing out loud that there were "two" trash cans in front of someone's house. Today, and every other day for some time, though, he just drones along as if marching to a funereal drum beat. At times, a passing stick or the sound of a lawn mower catches his fancy, but aside from these reactions he shows little animation. Even at our obligatory stop at the playground, he fails to show an interest in any of the equipment. He merely runs from piece to piece in a cacophony of movement.

Later that evening we receive a phone call from our doctor friend, Jeff. He has found another stone for us to overturn. A researcher in Washington, D.C., is experimenting with a drug called naltrexone. At this point, the preliminary results look promising, and, best of all, there are no known side effects. Curiously enough, the drug's safety record has been established from its long-term use with heroin addicts, a bit of ironic humor not lost on two former members of the counterculture.

Jeff is anxious to learn more about the study, so he offers to phone the researcher to get a better idea of the protocol and the feasibility of our participating. We agree to do the same and to alert the pediatrician as to our intentions.

Despite our relief at having another option to try, we aren't terribly enthusiastic about the prospects of this new drug. First of all, it has been found successful primarily in reducing self-abusive behavior. Since Jordan has manifested this kind of behavior only on the rare occasions when he has bitten his wrists, he doesn't stand to benefit much from its major effect. Second, we understand that the drug is supposed to work by blocking the uptake of natural opiates which, so the theory goes, will render the autistic person more sensitive to pain and other information-laden stimuli such as hugs and other physical contacts. This makes us doubly skeptical of its applicability to Jordan. He just doesn't fit the profile. He seems reasonably sensitive to pain and does not appear to be on the constant high which the researchers interested in this drug presume to be the case with at least a significant proportion of autistic individuals. And, finally, we are simply grown cynical of the "meds" approach to treating people with autism.

Never underestimate the capacity of the distressed for being led, however. In her initial conversation with Jill, the naltrexone researcher plays all the right cards. What it boils down to, she explains, is that autism is not going to be treatable through education, at least for the majority of those with the disorder. There is unquestionably a brain malfunction involved here: a physical malady which may be neurochemical or structural in origin. But the bottom line is that only a medical intervention is going to address the cause of the problem. So, forget the rest.

It is a convincing argument for which, given our analytical bent, we are ripe. Moreover, when we meet her in person, we are overwhelmed by the sheer weight of scientific rigor behind the study, as well as by her energy and personal presence. Here she is in beat-up basketball shoes and well-worn lab coat talking a steady, mile-a-minute, stream of neurochemicals and study results, appearing the down-to-earth genius who is about to translate the Rosetta stone. Pretty soon we're signing on the dotted line and off on another adventure.

From the outset, it is eminently clear that participating in this study will be tantamount to taking a part-time job. Each week, for several months, we will be driving the thirty-five miles to Washington at least once, to spend the better part of the day involved with activities related to the study. There will be baseline behavioral measures taken prior to Jordan's receiving the drug, there will be blood tests, there will be a mini-neurological evaluation for each session, and more. And before we can even take part in the study there will be yet another psychological evaluation to determine if Jordan is indeed a suitable subject.

Our participation in the study begins in August, so, because I am home, I am assigned to the first shift of visits running through Labor Day. Thereafter, Jill, with her thankfully flexible schedule, will be responsible for getting Jordan to the sessions. My first official act in advancing this particular piece of science takes place on a muggy Wednesday afternoon. I am to meet with the psychiatrist. As I sit in his office enduring the ordeal, I am acutely aware of a perception that had more or less come upon me several days before. It might be characterized this way. Before autism entered my life, I had what I would guess to be a typical stream of consciousness; that is to say that a rather normal volume of thoughts filled my mind from the commonplace sources. Now I have a river of consciousness; a big muddy of cerebrations swollen by tributaries of guilt, worry, anger, impatience, and dozens of other sources, themselves as big as rivers. At times it overspills its banks. At times it reacts with tremendous force that is difficult to control.

One of these times is now, in this doctor's office. It begins with the evaluation, which, for brevity, is unprecedented. A couple of questions, a few overtures directed at Jordan, and, yes, this is an autistic boy, suitable for study. Anger over this preconceived diagnosis barely has time to form, when I am engaged in the doctor's next line of inquiry, which focuses on our intentions regarding having other children. Now I am simultaneously annoyed at his audacity (this wasn't a genetic counseling session) and impatient with his story of a former student who had confided to him that having a handicapped sibling was one of the most inspiring experiences of her life. Spare me, Doc, I've read the *Reader's Digest* article! At the same time, though, I'm intensely interested in his reply to my concerns of recurrence. Jill and I have been anxious to have another child and have heard varying estimates of the chances of our having another child with autism. Heretofore, I have tended to believe the upper estimates, but this particular fellow makes the odds of recurrence seem so remote that I walk away from this visit feeling emboldened. Ironically, our daughter would be conceived within a week of this consultation.

It's hard to beat participating in a study, particularly a well-designed, rigorous study, for frustration. There are lengthy consent and background information forms to fill out, parking permits to be gotten, constant evaluations to be undergone, and then there are the idiosyncratic elements of each individual study which add to the fun. And if participating in this study seems difficult to us, it must seem an unbearable ordeal to Jordan.

First, there is the time commitment. Counting the two-hour drive, each session takes about six hours. Then you have the waiting periods: waiting for the neurologist, waiting for the behavioral observation period, waiting to have blood drawn, and so on. Then, of course, if you're three years old and a little confused by the world in the first place, having your blood drawn once a week must seem somewhat unpleasant. (Jordan's actual reaction to this experience was very frantic and heartbreaking to watch.) Add to this the half-hour period when he is separated from us and placed in a room with a stranger, so that we and the researcher can view and record the number and quality of attempts he makes to engage her socially, and you wind up with a pretty stress-inducing experience.

Around the second or third session of the study, I begin to sense how horrible Jordan feels about this process, and I'm almost overwhelmed with guilt. Since I've spoken to Jill about it already, I know she is feeling the same way. But what can we do? We aren't going to have the protocol changed on our account, and if we don't participate in the study, Jordan won't be able to take the drug, and we'll be once again without an option.

The matter comes to a head when something truly remarkable happens. At our fourth session in the study, Jordan is given about half a dose of the drug. This is the first time that he has been given anything close to the recommended level. During the session there isn't much of an observable effect, but things change dramatically around dinner time. That evening my brother-in-law and his wife are to come over for dinner. Shortly before they arrive, we notice that Jordan seems to be showing a modicum of purposefulness, playing semi-appropriately with a truck and his school bus. Later, at dinner, he seems to be in a better mood, more amenable to suggestions that he try a new food and willing to follow some simple directions. And after dinner he climbs our geodesic jungle gym set at the direction of his uncle with a joy and attentiveness we hadn't seen in months.

The thrill of hope fills our voices as we say goodbye to our company that evening. But the joy is tempered with the realization that it will be another week before Jordan gets this salubrious substance again. And, what's more, there are periods built into the study when he won't be receiving the drug at all. We don't want Jordan to be subjected to the tribulations of being a "once a week guinea pig," yet we want him to have the drug. We decide to retrace the path that we took with fenfluramine, that is, to ask Jeff to prescribe it for us.

Leaving this study proves to be a lot more difficult than we had expected. Everyone to whom we speak, including Jeff, seems incredulous that we're dropping out because we don't want Jordan to have to go through the regimen of the weekly visits. They particularly deprecate our concerns about Jordan's reaction to having his blood drawn weekly, pointing out that there is absolutely no evidence that this experience has any long term effects. But, then again, none of them have actually observed him during these sessions, and they may be underestimating the psychological effects of this experience on a child as vulnerable as Jordan. At any rate, nobody can give us a compelling reason for staying in the study other than that our withdrawing from it will negatively impact the research. And this isn't a sufficient reason to change our minds.

But the path to our decision is heavily scented with bad blood. Obviously, we have alienated the researcher by having wasted her time and reduced her sample size, and this will undoubtedly affect our relationship with a person whose work might one day prove helpful to Jordan. More importantly, we're not so self-centered as to be unmoved by the legitimate concerns that scientists, like this woman, express about being able to conduct well-controlled studies that will pass muster in a community of scholars. And we believe as much as she that conducting this kind of research is the best way that the various purposes of humanity will be served. So it is not lost on us that if too many people drop out of such efforts, a valuable source of information will have been lost. All that having been said, one still has to make decisions on a case-by-case basis. And, in this existential moment, we remain convinced that we're doing the right thing.

Our task then becomes one of convincing Jeff that he should somehow provide us with the naltrexone. Not without cause, he is not particularly happy with us at this point. He is a good doctor with no blemishes on his record, and he is more than a casual believer in the scientific method. All along he has thought that if we were going to try an unproven medical treatment it should occur in the framework of a controlled study. The fenfluramine incident, I believe, only served to strengthen that conviction. Now we're again asking him to do something that makes him uncomfortable, and that makes us extremely uncomfortable.

In the end, though, Jeff agrees. It would only be a guess, but I think three factors contributed most heavily to his decision. First, Jordan's age: Now three and a half, Jordan is in the critical period for language development. If naltrexone makes him more amenable to attending to his environment, there is at least an outside chance that he may begin to make significant gains in this area, and progress in this aspect of development would have an immense effect on his future. Second, is what I would call the "Bob Dylan factor," that is "if you ain't got nothin, you got nothin to lose." Just as we do, Jeff suspects that neither education nor psychotherapy holds much hope for improving Jordan, so the risks involved here seem clearly outweighed by the potential benefit, particularly if we have already seen some positive signs using the drug. And, finally, he seems to appreciate our concerns that the protocol for this study calls for extended periods of time when subjects get none or little of the drug. And, like us, he sub-scribes to the notion that time is of the essence.

If Jeff's annoyance with us for taking this step is muted due to friendship, our pediatrician is under no such con-straints. On a hot day in late summer, I am in the even more heated environment of an angry telephone conversation with an exasperated professional who believes his clients have gone off the deep end. It would have been bad enough if we had simply dropped out of the study, but to take it upon ourselves to play researchers with his patient, is more than he can stomach. And his thoughts bubble over into some pretty un-gentle territory. He suggests that our behavior is tantamount to child abuse. Just as angry, I respond by saying that we can't sit idly by while we think that there is something out there that can help Jordan now. I try to raise the issues of Jordan's

critical age and the fact that no major side effects are associated with the drug (actually, some concerns had been
raised by this time about potential liver damage associated
with taking naltrexone, but we had arranged through Jeff to
have this contingency monitored while Jordan is taking the
drug). I sense, though, as our conversation winds down, that
there is a gulf between us that will only be crossed when we
abandon what must seem to him a dangerous folly.

They say that history has a way of repeating itself, and our
experience with this erstwhile wonder drug could easily be advanced as evidence for that theory. Indeed, what happens
with naltrexone could quite reasonably be labelled
"Fenfluramine II." The story runs like this: There is no noticeable effect with varying dosages over a period of about two
weeks. If anything, Jordan seems to be getting more hyperactive and less responsive. For instance, it is during this period
that Jordan becomes unwilling to sit for meals. He also seems
more determined to shut us out, often forcing us to raise our
voices to a shout to get his attention. Since the drug doesn't
seem to help, we decide that continuing with it just isn't
worth the risk. Drugs won't be our ticket out of hell.

Strange as it may seem after all these setbacks, we aren't
totally crushed by the experience with naltrexone. One reason
we may be responding more optimistically, is that we now
know that Jill is pregnant again. Although we have obvious
and legitimate concerns of recurrence, neither of us is thinking that such an event is likely, and if the amnio doesn't
reveal anything—especially if it's a girl—we are convinced
that only good things can come from it.

Another factor which makes life easier for us during this
period is our decision to hire two college students to work
with Jordan on a regular basis. In our continuous ponderings
about what might bring Jordan out of his shell, we have more

than once considered the possibility of using amateur or professional play therapists, and we get more serious about the idea as we begin to notice that Jordan frequently responds better to people other than us. We're looking for folks who would have, not only an interest in working with a different kind of kid, but also the energy and creativity necessary to catch that type of kid's attention. With these credentials in mind, we post a notice on a local college bulletin board.

Patti and Therese, the two graduate students who respond to the notice, begin working several hours a week with Jordan at the tail end of the summer. Therese mainly plays with Jordan at our house. She tries to interest him in dolls, trucks, and other toys used for social play. Patty plays with Jordan at her apartment. She involves him more in arts and crafts, music, and cooking. The common thread of their approach is a very low pressure and gentle demeanor with Jordan. Each continues this arrangement over a period of about five months.

What these women bring to us is more than mere time off from a child whose behavior is becoming increasingly stressful. They also act as a sounding board for the various ideas and concerns that we share about Jordan which we can't always effectively communicate to our friends and relatives or the professionals with whom we are consulting. In a very palpable sense they are in a unique position to be good listeners and to share their own insights, being less prone to the emotive reaction of a person close to us, and also less apt to view things from the limited perspective of the professional. Therese is especially good at noticing things that get a positive reaction from Jordan. We use many of her suggestions to attract and hold Jordan's attention.

A third factor which facilitates stability during the fall is our increasing involvement in activities unrelated to Jordan. I am once again back at work and am also in the process of putting together a thesis proposal for my doctorate. And Jill has begun to take on more hours and responsibilities in her job too. We therefore have fewer opportunities to see Jordan and less time to think about him.

And finally, there remains the residue of hope from previous medical consultations and our review of the literature which suggested that Jordan was in the best prognosis group—a hope, which when combined with Jordan's unusual developmental history, makes it seem impossible that he won't again begin to progress.

But this period of relative calm and confidence masks our continuing vulnerability. Rather than equilibrium, our state is more like suspended animation, from which the slightest pressure from without could precipitate a fall. And things begin to change as we move toward the end of our first year with autism.

III

"How can they possibly think that this is going to help Jordan? There isn't a single kid in the class like him. And all they do is force him to participate in every activity. There doesn't even seem to be a plan for him." Jill rambles on as I sit at the kitchen table silently nodding. She proceeds to relate the details of her visit to observe Jordan's class—one of the many she would make over the four-month period that Jordan attends the early childhood special education class provided by our county. Jordan is now a full-time student in a class of developmentally delayed children, meaning he attends school five days a week and receives more ancillary services such as speech therapy.

She goes on: "They haven't the slightest idea of how to motivate him, and without that they can't take him anywhere."

"Maybe it takes time. You know, to build a relationship," I reply unconvincingly. I notice a big frown sweeping across Jill's face and move quickly to avoid the impending breaker. "Well, none of us have come up with the answer to Jordan's recalcitrance. He's a hard nut to crack."

"That's just it, Craig. We can't rely on some public school class where he's thrown in with everyone from kids with cerebral palsy to kids with Down syndrome. It's just not going to work, and we've got to do something to make it happen for him before it's too late. That's why I think we need to do this Kaufman thing. They realize that motivation must come from within, and they can help us find ways to tap into what turns Jordan on." Without waiting for a response, Jill gathers her keys and purse and heads out the door to pick up Jordan from Patti's.

I hear the car back out of the driveway as I look out on the bare trees in the back yard. It's a cool, damp day in early November, and the sky and the trees seem to share the same color of gray. The silence of the house covers me like an uncomfortable fabric. And as if to fill the cloying quiet, disjointed fragments of thought well up from within, screeching across my consciousness. I try to summarize my situation: I have an autistic child, a child who by all my advisors' accounts should be progressing, but isn't; I have another child on the way; I have a wife who is becoming desperately dissatisfied with the status quo, and who now wants to begin an intensive at-home program of therapy based solely on the work of a former ad executive's experiences with his own and one other autistic child—work which, though highly publicized, has not won widespread scientific acclaim.

And I must add yet other elements to this simmering cerebral stew. The Kaufman program, in which we seem destined to participate, is not without its costs. First, there's the money—over $9,000 for the anticipated two-week training which we would receive. Then, there's the little matter of having an educational program run from our home fourteen hours a day, seven days a week. There's also the matter of recruiting volunteers to help us give the intensive one-on-one therapy that the program calls for. Not to mention the impact on one or both of our careers as we take indefinite leaves of absence to run the program.

On the face of it, it seems a simple decision: to undertake such an activity in mid career, with a new baby on the way and very few potential volunteers to help us manage, seems impossible. But take the contrary position, as my wife so ably does in her profession as a lawyer. What if we don't act? We feel certain that Jordan isn't going to improve in his current placement, and there are no other options available to us.

What will be easier to stomach in the long run: to try something which seems modestly dubious and fail, or to sit idly by wringing our hands as our child drifts into an abyss like an untethered astronaut falling into the blackness of space? For me it comes down to Jill's mental state. No matter how well or ill this undertaking serves us, it will surely be better for her to have taken direct action on behalf of her child. Fait accompli!

By now, though, the reader may be asking herself about the limits of our credulity. For in this period of a single earth revolution around the sun, we have tried behavior modification, pet therapy, play therapy, and two unsanctioned drugs. And we have also not been above issuing exhortations from the agnostic's prayerbook. Lest you judge too harshly, however, you must remember this rule, in case it ever applies to you: Credulity is an elastic element, capable of stretching in proportion with need.

There is a story from my wife's family, which over the years has taken on the character of a parable, that relates well here. It goes like this: at a family reunion some years back my father-in-law misplaced his camera. Not given to losing things, and less given to parting with a hard-earned dollar without a fight, he launched an exhaustive search for his camera that lasted the better part of an afternoon. At one point, he passed by a cooler in an area that he had already searched several times. To my sister-in-law's amazement, he opened the cooler to look inside for the camera. In her incredulousness she made the mistake of remarking, "But Kabe, surely you don't think the camera could be in there!" Without hesitating to ponder the obvious, he simply replied, "That was an expensive camera!"

In going out on this thin limb, we may be in search of the camera in the cooler, but this is our child. Besides, much of what the Kaufmans say in *Son Rise* and *A Miracle to Believe In*, the two books describing their work with autistic children, confirms our own experiences, making it that much easier to suspend the empirical habit of mind. Thus when they talk of the inadequacy of behavior modification, or the cold, hyper-rationality of the professionals, or the futility of drugs, they meet squarely with all that has taken place in our own lives over the past eleven months. Add to this the feeling of empowerment that comes from knowing that you are taking matters into your own hands, and the idea of "curing" your child through intensive, loving attention becomes not only attractive, but absolutely irresistible. ❃

❃

❃

❃

❃ I have been standing at the kitchen window lost in an unseeing gaze for half an hour, pondering the impact of our impending experiment with home therapy for Jordan, when I realize that it has gotten dark, and I've become stiff. Jill is not yet home from Patti's, so I surmise that she has taken him to the mall or the grocery store, a task which takes a bit of courage of late due to his proclivity to tantrum in such places. Dinner has already been prepared, so I decide to listen to music for a while.

Over the past several weeks I have developed a bit of an obsession with a certain kind of music—sad. For some reason or other, it has been very helpful for me to lie absolutely still for periods of up to an hour just soaking in the somber tones or lyrics of a variety of compositions. My tastes are eclectic, requiring only the common variable of melancholia for approval. The selections for this particular session are exemplary: *The Pachelbel Canon* and Bruce Springsteen's *The River*.

Frozen on the floor as the night darkens the dining room around me, I slip into the images the music evokes. First, the crushing drudgery of an imaginary seventeenth-century life, brought into relief by the doleful groans of the cellos and double basses. Then the apocalyptic visions of a post-industrial working class existence, drawn out with electric guitars and Springsteen's haunting voice.

But isn't something wrong here? My home is the three-bedroom rancher of the modern American suburb, where Bogeymen are banned. I worked hard, I kept my nose to the grindstone, I flew away from the poverty and parochialism of my working-class background on the back of a sheepskin only to find myself back where I started. This music serves as my reminder that an escape in space and time is only relative, the principal emotions of this existence remain absolute: and in a land of recurring human sadness, my passport is good. ❅

❅

❅

❅

❅ My wistful mood is broken as the door swings open, and Jordan rushes in. Jill follows, out of breath, holding a heavy bag of groceries. "How many times do I have to listen to that morose music?" she comments as she hands me the bag and busies herself with setting the table. "You're going to get yourself into the same kind of funk you were in last year."

"No, I just find this kind of music soothing for now. I don't feel any more depressed than usual, and I'm certainly not as sad as I was when we found out about Jordan. Actually, sad music makes me realize how much a part of life sadness is, and having that thought before me may make me less prone to self-pity." Seeing how this explanation plays to, at best, a tepid response, I change the subject. "How was your trip to the store?"

"Awful. He screamed and flailed going in, and continued to be unhappy for just about the whole time we were there," Jill answers despondently. She arranges the plates and directs me to wash Jordan's hands while she sets all the food on the table.

"Good thing you got to the store," I remark, noticing the new bottle of barbecue sauce strategically placed in front of Jordan. "Now Jordan will be able to get through the meal, secure in the thought that there will be sufficient chemical alteration of his food to make it edible. Shall we try to get him to eat some of it without the sauce?"

"Not on your life. I've already been through enough battles today. I want to save some energy for bedtime." We share a knowing glance after this remark, as here, encapsuled in this brief pre-dinner scene, are the three most salient themes of our life with Jordan in the late fall of 1985: battles over a severely restricted diet, temper tantrums in public places, and a rapidly deteriorating sleeping pattern that threatens to bring us all to the brink of exhaustion. In saying that she wants to conserve her energy for bedtime, Jill is reflecting on the greater than chance probability that tonight will find us waking in the middle of the night to find Jordan jumping up and down on the bed and making noises. One of us will then have to bundle him into the car and drive for as much as an hour until he falls soundly enough asleep to remain in that state for the rest of the night. Indeed, for a period of almost a year, Jordan would wake up in the middle of the night at least three times a week, requiring one or both of us to spend a minimum of an hour settling him down. When I recall that this period coincided with the bulk of Jill's pregnancy and the first three months of our daughter's life, I can barely believe that Jill survived. ❄

❄

❄

❄

❄ Sleigh bells ring. We aren't listening. In the lane, nothing's glistening. It's Christmas in the land of autism, a time which later would aptly be referred to as the "Hellidays" by a friend who also has a child with autism. For the parents of a seriously handicapped child it is a time when you are flooded with emotions. Along with the heavy baggage of negative feelings you carry throughout the year, you must carefully load the celebratory spirit of the season on your psyche. Well-meaning relatives and friends want to create situations to "cheer you up." You receive gifts. You are bombarded with happy music and bright decorations. There is simply no way for you to avoid the dichotomies between the world that you now inhabit and the one that you left. And, laden with the weight of inauthentic emotions which must receive public expression, that psyche creaks and groans and sometimes eventually collapses.

If your child's disability is autism, other funny plums get into the Christmas pie. Take for instance, the purchasing of Christmas presents. Jordan has no imaginative play skills and very little self-organization, so what toys do you buy for him? And buying all clothes seems strange too. Then there's the matter of opening his presents—we do it for him since he screams if we attempt to involve him. The whole Christmas morning process thus becomes the shadow of an act whose participants are only present in body. Yet, for some reason, it seems necessary to proceed with the charade. ❋

❋

❋

❋

❋ It is the shortest day of the year, and the house is already dark when I return home from work on the last day of school before Christmas vacation. The phone is ringing as I enter, and I fumble my way to the receiver. My heart stops when the voice on the other end tells me she's calling from the lab that has done the amniocentesis. "Dear God, tell me everything is all right," I breathe as I await her comments. "Everything's fine? That's wonderful. Yes, I'm very interested in knowing the sex. A girl? Bless you for calling before Christmas; this is going to make things a lot merrier around here."

I'm hardly off the phone when it rings again. It's Jill calling from work, wondering if I'd heard the very news that has just been delivered. We share a cosmic leap for joy and a long-distance embrace, realizing that we just got the only Christmas present we wanted. Even though we know that having a girl is still no guarantee of not having another autistic child, we figure our odds have been somewhat reduced, since boys are four times as likely to develop autism. We are also relieved to know that the other birth defects for which the test screens can be ruled out.

Our holiday joy is short lived, though. It isn't long before Jordan's presence at the family get-togethers becomes problematic for everyone. The crowds make him even more desperate for the shrinking personal space he so craves. He refuses to participate in the least of holiday activities. And everyone is visibly uncomfortable balancing their desire to show us support with their natural inclinations to pity us. We wind up avoiding some of the festivities altogether, which creates friction between Jill and her mother and sets a "holiday on thin ice" tone for the rest of the week.

On top of all this, there remain serious questions about the wisdom of our impending trip to the Kaufman's Option Institute, discussions about which have at times been heated. There is by no means consensus regarding the benefit of a two-week training program which will cost us in excess of $9,000. The logistical concerns also present problems for those uninitiated to the sense of futility we are feeling about Jordan. Many with whom we would speak during that holiday season appreciated our dilemma, but they also questioned the feasibility of our plan. And, in Jill's eyes, partial allegiance would not be enough. ❄

❄

❄

❄

❄ "Nothing is good or bad but thinking makes it so." So goes the line from Shakespeare; and so the thinking of Barry and Suzy Kaufman, founders of the Option Institute and self-styled autism therapists. For a year now we have been reading of the Kaufmans' work as well as getting information about them from other sources. We have also spent some time talking to Suzy Kaufman about her philosophy of working with autistic children. Now, on this cold January night, we are pulling into their vast complex straddling the border between

Massachusetts and Connecticut. We are about to receive
training from the people who claim that autism can be
"cured" through intensive love and extensive work.

Why have we come here? What brings two people who
have traditionally required scientific evidence from those who
would prove a point to a place that advertises miracles? Has
desperation so clouded our thinking that we are at the mercy
of every shaman and quack who would commend to the
public their wares? Well, not exactly. It is true that the Kaufmans do not receive the endorsement of any professional organization involved in the treatment of autism. And it is
further true that they don't provide prospective clients with
an expansive list of references. (In fact, their own son and an
unnamed Mexican boy are the only children they claim to
have "cured.") And it could be fairly said that they have insu-
lated themselves from the oversight of the scientific community. But, all that aside, there are elements of their
approach which either make sense intuitively, or have been
found effective in other settings.

For example, their recognition that any successful educational or psychological treatment of autism would require tons
of intense man-hours has been subsequently confirmed by the
research of Ivar Lovaas and others. Also, their apprehension
of the critical role that family members play in any therapy
has become well established among professionals. Additionally, specific features of their methodology, such as imitating the
behavior of autistic children in order to get their attention,
have been found to work in other settings. When all of this is
combined with the fact that none of our advisers has been
openly critical of our decision to seek counsel from the Kaufmans, then what we are about to do seems rational.

We're hardly out of the car when one of the staff emerges
from the little house that is to be our home for the next two

weeks. She greets us in a manner that is so disarmingly sunny that it takes me back a little. My Teutonic background betrays me in these situations where immediate affection is called for, and, to my chagrin, the customs of our hosts will not deviate from this "hug a stranger" line throughout our stay. What's more, there is a kind of homogenous demeanor among all who work or study at the institute that puts me in mind of the line from "Home on the Range" about seldom hearing a discouraging word. It's not long before I begin to sense that life here is so infused with this conspiracy of celebration that the motto might well be: "Abandon all despair, ye who enter here." Well, what did I expect from the "Place for Miracles?"

In the morning, it becomes apparent to us how well these New Age gurus of special education are living. A prodigious mansion, a sprawling campus, a stable of hired hands—now I know how they can justify that $4,500 a week consulting tab. There's a ton of overhead here, even if they are paying their staff squat. So opulent are the surroundings, that I get an uneasy feeling as Jill and I trudge up the hill to the Kaufman mansion to receive our orientation from Suzy. My level of discomfort only increases as we enter the study. A massive bookcase stocked with the classic texts of the Human Potential Movement stares out over the plush carpet. A faint tinkle of bells and a whisper of Tibetan muzac hover around the room. For a moment, I am transported to my college days of fifteen years past when, among other cognoscenti of the counterculture, I awaited—consciousness altered—the dawn of a new era. And throughout my two-week stay at the Kaufmans', I am reminded again and again of a period in my life that for ten years had been but a distant memory.

In retrospect, the most apparent similarity between these two periods lies in what they seemed to offer—release. As a naive practitioner of radical politics during the late sixties, I

imagined that the efforts of the faithful would put an entirely
different face on issues such as the influence of the military-in-
dustrial complex, racial and sexual injustice, and the degrada-
tion of the environment. It might take hard work, but
inevitably our "voice of reason" could not fail to bring us into
an era of unparalleled harmony. The Option Institute's staff
won't make promises of that dimension, but they do maintain
that release from unhappiness about what fate has given me is
imminent, if only my attitude toward life changes. Like the
hippies of the 1960s, the Kaufmans issue a huge line of credit
for change on the minimal collateral of simple faith. Thus,
while the radicals of the earlier era might think it impossible
for corruption and deceit to rule in the light of day that would
shine from their ideas, the Kaufmans and their followers take
it as an article of faith that one can merely pronounce any circumstance happy and it will be so.

On several instances, in fact, Suzy or other staff members
related discussions they had held with former clients as a way
of bringing home this very point. A typical scenario had them
reforming the misguided position of a distraught father who
claimed that he would never be happy with changing the
diapers of his elementary school aged child. Perhaps, in the
end, this poor chap recovered from his convoluted thinking
that every situation isn't equally conducive to joy.

Another way that our experience with the Kaufmans is
reminiscent of the days of "fear and loathing" of our youth is
the living conditions. As in college, we are living in a dor-
mitory-like setting with tiny rooms in a house that accom-
modates not only us but several students and workers as well.
We eat our meals cafeteria-style with the folks who are serving as our mentors. Much of the discussion at those meals and
in other settings around the institute centers on the activities
and ideas that arise there. Here again, like old times.

The surroundings, the philosophy, the esprit de corps—
they all take me back to another time in my life, but there are
also distinct differences between the experiences and atmosphere of this place and those of my college days. As students
we were force-fed a diet of realist literature, existential
philosophy, and liberal to radical politics by academics who
saw it as their duty to create in their charges an attitude of
skepticism. At the Option Institute, on the other hand, there
are no texts, save the books and tapes of Barry Kaufman, and
the staff go out of their way to avoid taking stands on any
issue for fear of committing the cardinal sin of the place: being
judgmental. And, finally, in the old days we questioned everything from marriage to money, but at the institute they accept
the world as given in its entirety while all the while probing
us with endless questions regarding our feelings about literally
hundreds of hypothetical situations.

I have digressed. This rambling journey began as we
entered the study of Barry (a.k.a. Bears) and Suzy Kaufman.
What jumps out at me when I first meet Suzy Kaufman that
morning is that she is a consummate teacher. And like all
great practitioners of that art, she follows some basic rules:
keep it simple, do a lot of repetition, make it fun, and provide
adequate feedback. All toothy grin and movement, she boun-
ces from topic to topic, all the while getting a feel for her new
pupils. This is ostensibly an orientation meeting, but Suzy uses
it to lay out her views on everything from the nature of autism
to the path to happiness. This is not a woman whose mind has
been dimmed by spending hundreds of hours in a bathroom
with an autistic child.

Although the conversation is far ranging on this first
morning at the institute, we do get an idea of what to expect
over the next two weeks. The program will consist of the following components: observations of the staff working with Jor-

dan, working ourselves with Jordan, getting feedback from the
staff about our sessions with Jordan, getting feedback from
each other, getting feedback from the staff on our manner of
giving feedback, general one-on-one counseling sessions with
Suzy and various staff, and group discussions to share information on the various sessions that everyone has had with Jordan. It's a complete agenda with very little free time. Even my
daily run has to be fit in during the time allotted for lunch.

We begin the process early on Monday morning with our
first observation of an Option Institute worker. Steve is an experienced practitioner of the Kaufman method and has, we
are told, worked with many disabled children. He exhibits
great enthusiasm as he takes Jordan into a large playroom
stocked with toys, puzzles, and other objects designed to cap-
ture the interest of a young child. Jill, Suzy, and I sit outside
the room and observe through a window, taking notes as we
watch.

Inside, Steve has a good bit of difficulty getting Jordan's
attention. Jordan seems more interested in leaving the scene
than in playing with any of the toys. He keeps going to the
door and trying to open it. Steve successfully redirects his attention away from the door a number of times, and, after a
while, Jordan stops focusing on the exit. He still, however,
doesn't show much interest in Steve. During the hour or so
that Steve is with Jordan, he manages to get some interaction
by tickling him. He also gets Jordan to walk on some large
blocks, using them as stepping stones, but not much more.

In the feedback period that follows Steve's session, Suzy
stresses the attitudinal components of Steve and Jordan's interaction. The lesson for us to absorb is that a session is a time
for gaining Jordan's trust by expressing verbally and nonverbal-
ly an unconditional affection for him. There is no agenda of
skills that Jordan should be working on, and there is no

timetable for his "recovery." In fact, the staff at the Institute would repeatedly impress on us their belief that Jordan was just fine the way he was. Their theme would run something like, "You can want Jordan to behave more normally, but he can be seen as beautiful even if he doesn't change."

Besides fleshing out the feelings part of Steve's session with Jordan, Suzy examines her notes to point out those incidents where Jordan seemed to show interest or communicate. A great deal of significance is placed on developing a kind of compendium of activities that motivate Jordan. The Kaufmans' position seems to be that Jordan is capable of communicating and learning, but will only do so when he is shown that the world is safe and interesting.

The feedback sessions as well as the training on how to give feedback are driven by the notion that a person grows in the Option process through self-examination. Accordingly, these sessions are highlighted by questions rather than comments. "How did you feel when. . . ?" "Was there something that kept you from pursuing that activity?" These types of questions that require more than short answers are frequently raised. There is no issue that can't be raised by the person or persons conducting the feedback, but making judgmental statements is strongly discouraged.

Not long into the program, we are doing our own sessions with Jordan. They seem to go pretty much like those the Option staffers do. In imitation of our tutors, we frequently make dramatic gestures such as jumping off chairs. We talk to Jordan almost constantly, and in loud tones. We offer copious praise, encouraging him with comments such as, "Wow, Jordan, you made a great tower," or, "That was great the way you looked right at me." When he allows, we also get physical by tickling, swinging, and dancing with him. If he protests or shows some discomfort with any of these activities, however,

we stop immediately, in keeping with the philosophy of letting Jordan decide what will not take place in the sessions. On
the other hand, if Jordan makes a request for anything (and he
frequently does indicate a desire for apples or other food
items), it is honored right away.

The group sessions are more clinical. At these meetings,
all of the people working with Jordan (other than the person
who is with him at the time) get together to come up with
ideas related to practical problems, such as what to do about
Jordan's persistent requests to leave the room. Each par-
ticipant also gets to discuss things that he has noticed about
Jordan's behavior. Everything is still pretty free-form, though,
and no game plan of how to work with Jordan emerges from
these discussions.

In summary, the Option program calls for isolating the
child in a room with one person at a time for all of the child's
waking hours. According to the theory, it is necessary to keep
the child in an enclosed space in order to minimize potential
distractions that might reduce his ability to attend to the person who is with him. Optimally, a series of people—family
members and other volunteers—work in a series of sessions
lasting approximately two hours each. The main objective for
the person conducting the session is to make the child so comfortable in his presence that he would begin to interact spontaneously with the "therapist." These kinds of interactions
would then lead to the child becoming more normal socially
and cognitively, thus ending the need for the program.

All the activity associated with Option is a little disorient-
ing for the first few days, but around the fourth or fifth day I
get a sense that I understand the lay of the land. And it's pretty uneven terrain. On the plus side, it's undeniable that the
energy and enthusiasm of the staff have motivated us to work
harder and feel more hopeful about Jordan. It's also clear that

our mentors have good ideas about working with autistic children. Moreover, they know how to help us build on the ideas that we generate. If, for example, we notice something that really seems to motivate Jordan, they persist in questioning us until we come up with related activities that we might try in a subsequent session. But there are many features of the training that are utterly tiresome, and as the days go by they become energy suckers. Most notable among the negative aspects of the Option program are the one-on-one self counseling sessions. These generally take place over hour-long walks with one of the staffers, during which we are flooded with questions about our feelings. The purpose of these seems to be to help clients come to grips with issues which might interfere with the functioning of their programs. Such issues might include personal attitudes that impede optimal effort, doubts about the feasibility of running an option program once one has returned home, or beliefs that simply make one unhappy. The thinking appears to be that if you are experiencing negative feelings of one sort or another, the child or the other people working in the program will pick it up. This in turn will poison the relationships and undermine the program.

As we take part in this part of the program, I occasionally think that the assumptions which are the scaffolding for these sessions are, at least in part, unwarranted. For example, how likely is it that a child who makes minimal eye contact and has serious receptive language deficits is picking up those subtle cues from the behavior of others which reflect their attitudes? But, for argument's sake, let's say that that assumption is correct. Does it necessarily follow that responding to an unending string of questions from someone you have just met will put you sufficiently at ease to keep you in a happy frame of mind? My personal experience suggests to me that my moods are not amenable to this kind of fine tuning. But even if we assume that I can be made a happier, less judgmental person through this Socratic self-examination process, does that mean that Jordan will, or even can, choose to respond to this loving treatment by emerging from his autism?

There are exponential leaps of faith here which are spawned by the Kaufmans' extreme existential stand, according to which we are free not only to be the author of our life's work, but to be its critic as well. We can judge—or more appropriately suspend judgment on—ourselves, others, and every act in the universe. And it all can be pronounced a happy state of affairs. Never mind that you are obese, stupid, devoid of personality, or whatever, you can achieve a full measure of happiness by simply telling yourself that you are so. What's more, that license applies not only to the sound of mind. Even the child with autism can actually choose to enter the world as a full and happy partner, provided that he is properly motivated.

What allows the Kaufmans to plant this unproven seed of free will in the most hostile of soils, is their reliance on the argument from extreme cases. Thus, for example, if you question your ability to maintain your happiness, or even your sanity, in the face of life with an autistic child, they will counter with stories of Holocaust survivors who kept up their spirits under exceedingly inhumane conditions. Or should you doubt the ability of your severely handicapped child to choose not to exhibit autistic behavior, they can point to the examples of the two children that they "cured." What is missing from the Option philosophy is a recognition of the laws of probability. ❉

❉

❉

❉

❊ It would be nice if I could express my feelings about this experience openly, I think as I glance away from the counselor during yet another one-on-one session. No sooner do I make this inadvertent display of inattentiveness, though, then the counselor, like some high school girlfriend eager for attention, pounces on me with a question about what I am thinking. I want to say "lunch," but I am what my high school baseball coach would call "coachable," what my teachers would call "teachable," what my mother would call "controllable." At this point in my life I'm still too well-mannered to tell this woman that I'm tired of this exercise. Besides, should I admit of such a feeling, who knows where it might lead? Instead, I create a phony "issue" for us to chew on for the remainder of our walk, and ponder lunch.

Back at our living quarters, I see Jill finishing up her walk with Suzy. We decide to take a peek in on Jordan before we head to lunch. He is "working" with Charles, our favorite of the institute's staff. Charles has a block balanced on his nose and is, at the same time, calling Jordan's attention to his antics. For his part, Jordan seems more interested in lunch, looking, as he is, at the door and repeating, "I want apple."

Jill and I exchange a smile at this scene and head out toward the eatery. Along the way, she is rattling off superlatives about Suzy's ability to counsel. I'm a little edgy. I don't share her enthusiasm, but I can't play this bad hand now. I have to be careful about my feelings. Like those overlay drawings of the various systems of the body depicted in biology texts, I must place my feelings about this situation carefully over those of Jill and the other players involved, or the picture won't come out right. Partial enthusiasm, however, is the most easily discernible of emotions, and it isn't long before Jill is confronting me with my lack of total commitment to the impending program. During our initial week here we have been too busy for feeling each other out about what we're going through. Our days have been full, and in the evenings we have taken turns doing sessions with Jordan. But on the weekends our time is our own, and the increased responsibility for being with Jordan as well as the additional time we have alone with each other (that is, apart from the institute's staff) prove to be a volatile mix.

I have doubts about the legitimacy of this therapy which, during our weekend discussions, become difficult to hide. I wonder out loud why the staff here isn't more free with names of folks who are currently doing this kind of program. I have trouble accepting their notion that Jordan must stay in a room for who knows how long until he has recovered. And I question the feasibility of our undertaking such an operation, especially with a new baby due in less than four months. Jill, on the other hand, thinks that anything short of complete and immediate replication of what the Kaufmans are suggesting to us would render the solution totally ineffective. She makes the cogent point of questioning my rationale for agreeing to pay these people handsome sums of money while proceeding to relegate their positions to those of opinion—no better than my own. And she goes on to speculate whether my indecisiveness here doesn't hold great room for doubt about my ability to organize a program once we get home.

It's back and forth this way over the weekend during those times that others are working with Jordan and we are free to talk. By Sunday night it is clear that Jill will accept nothing less than the total package. I decide that going through this experience is what is meant to be if we are to stay

together and, further, that developing an accepting attitude
about it might bring dividends regardless of its impact on Jordan. What are a few more slightly inauthentic acts in a
human existence fraught with such acts, after all?

So, during the second week at the institute, I take my
place on Shakespeare's "living stage," and begin to better play
my part in the unfolding drama. Actually, as the week progresses I begin to feel more comfortable with the impending
enterprise. Jordan has made some slight improvements, such
as more frequent and longer eye contact, and we begin to get a
better handle on the logistics of how we will set up our
program. Additionally, the staff at the institute becomes more
involved with issues of practical concern to us. By the end of
the week I'm once again feeling confident that this is something that makes sense—for now.

On a brilliant and frigid afternoon we take our leave of
Suzy Kaufman, our beguiling and clever guide through the "option" process. Suzy is full of accolades for our efforts and insights; attributes which she is certain will serve us well in
motivating Jordan to rejoin the human race. We respond in
kind with praise for the inspirational quality of her work and
that of the staff. Caught up in the moment, I even refer to the
option philosophy as "existentialism with a happy ending."
That, of course, will remain to be seen.

Being adroit marketers of their service, the Kaufmans ask
one final favor of us as we leave: that we write down our
thoughts about the experience at the institute before we go
home. Having both enthusiasm for and reservations about
their work, I come up with the only idea which I think fairly
summarizes the value of this method whose outcome has yet
to be tested. It is the biblical saying: "You will know them by

their fruits." If the Option Institute experience helps a parent of a special needs child either to improve the functioning of that child or to better accept his level of functioning, then it has yielded bountiful fruit. If it does not, then it is a different kind of seed.

On Saturday morning, I hand our "report card" to the woman who welcomed us two weeks earlier as we pile into the car for the long trip home. There's a final hug and then, trailing clouds of questions, we are on our way into another new life. Having spent the last two weeks confined to two rooms, Jordan seems stunned when we open the door and let him outside. For nearly the entire ride home he gazes out the window in apparent amazement at the scenery and the cars passing by. He has also become unaccustomed to the cold and acts as if we're dragging him across the frozen tundra whenever we leave the car for meals and rest stops. Perhaps because of the novelty, Jordan is very pleasant throughout the long journey back to Maryland, and we take that as an omen of good things to come.

When we aren't interacting with Jordan we spend the bulk of our time in the car finalizing our game plan for the home program. We estimate that we'll need between fifteen and twenty helpers. We are operating under the assumption that most of our volunteers will only want to do one two-hour session per week. If fifteen people work with us, that will cover thirty hours, and Jill and I will cover the remaining forty hours. Extra volunteers might be needed to fill in when the regulars miss a session.

"Let's see," Jill says as she pulls a little pad out of her purse. "We'll have Mom and Dad, Jim and Kathy, and Therese [the graduate student play therapist who has agreed to stay on with us in this program]. That makes five. We might also be able to get Jan [a college friend]. And you know how many people she knows. I bet that some of Kathy's teacher and student friends would be interested in something like this, too. If we can get five out of that group, five college students, and four or five high school kids, we'll be in great shape."

I predict that some of my old graduate school mentors might also help us get college students (at this time I was in my final year in a Ph.D. program at the University of Maryland). "I can't believe that we wouldn't get a few interested parties if they made announcements in their classes," I say. "And high school students should be even easier to get."

Given our many contacts, we both agree that getting help for the long run shouldn't be a problem. But there will be a two-week period during which we'll be extremely strapped. It will take at least this long before I'm able to secure a leave of absence, and Jill is scheduled to work until right before the baby is due. That means that one of us will have to take off additional time to begin the program with Jordan. Because this kind of activity is strenuous, it would be best for that person to be me, but I'm afraid that taking off additional time might jeopardize my leave of absence, so the onus falls on Jill. We agree to enlist heavy support from my in-laws and hope that they'll be willing to take on yet another burden.

So much to think about. So much to do. A line of gray-black clouds sheathe the sky as we approach our house. Beside me Jill is holding Jordan on her lap and talking softly into the back of his head. As he has been for most of the trip, Jordan is sitting still and staring straight ahead. In his profile I see the same little turned-up nose that jumps out from the photo of Jill at age five that I carry in my wallet. From as early as ten months his face has been her face; his rapid early development like the stories I have heard of Jill's; the impact of his presence on my life the same as that of his mother's. God, you couldn't have meant for the comparison to end here! ❄

❄

❄

❄

❄ There isn't any time to lose when we get home. We want to begin briefing people right away, so the very first night we're eating with the in-laws, explaining to them the option process and laying out the game plan. I sense from their reaction that no salesman need call: they will be full partners in this enterprise. The next night we have Jill's brother and his wife over, and they too offer to pitch in. Before the week is out we have notices placed on college bulletin boards and in the local high school guidance office. And we have called friends and spoken to neighbors and acquaintances from work, all the while maintaining a twelve-hour-a-day program for Jordan.

In many ways this period is reminiscent of the same time last year. We are, once again, busy to distraction. But whereas last year we were simply running from place to place getting information, or reading everything we could get our hands on, now we have a plan of action. After we notify the public school officials that Jordan will not be returning, we begin converting his room into a playroom and move his bedding into the spare bedroom. We also begin meeting with people who are interested in working in the program. We have the most success attracting high school students, and within a three-week period six of these enthusiastic idealists are working alongside us. Our college friend Jan also agrees to become involved, and she enlists the help of two of her friends as well.

By the time our program is fully operational, we have fifteen people helping us.

By the standards we had set for the operation before we got started, this beginning is auspicious. We would have liked to have had more college students involved, and we would have preferred that more of the people working with us would be doing so on a volunteer basis, but for the level of excitement among the participants and for the ease of setting up the schedules and other parameters of the program, things couldn't have gone much better. What's more, the training seems to go incredibly well. With one or two exceptions, everyone appears tuned in to the concept of the therapy and able to carry out their sessions with Jordan with a minimum of supervision after only a single observation and trial session.

Another big concern is taken care of when my leave comes through without a hitch. And by the last week of February I am the head honcho of the program, responsible for doing about six hours a day with Jordan, as well as conducting some cursory feedback on other people's sessions and helping Jill with the scheduling. Imagine yourself a combination cheerleader, adolescent counselor, housewife, and volunteer coordinator for twelve hours a day, and you get some idea of what I'm experiencing. This is the stuff of burn-out. Waking at six in the morning to grab forty-five minutes for breakfast and the paper, doing two to three hours with Jordan until Carol or Kabe relieves me for an hour and a half, going back in with Jordan for another ninety minutes until Jim or one of the high school kids relieves me again (I usually use this break to run), and completing a final session of about an hour before the high school students, Jill, and the other volunteers finish up the day. Sandwiched in between the sessions done in the late afternoon and evening are Jordan's meal preparation, conversations with the various workers regarding Jordan's progress, attempts to recruit other volunteers, and work on my dissertation.

Jill's life is even more hectic, consisting of all of the above except the dissertation plus a full-time job. And she's in the final trimester of her pregnancy!

As I enter the house after my run, I hear Michelle's soprano voice reverberating around the walls as she pursues Jordan around the perimeter of the session room. One of our high school students, Michelle is a vivacious and tireless worker whose sessions with Jordan are always all-out affairs. And she enhances her fever pitch efforts with a wardrobe from which you could make a paint chart. Today it's hot pink pants with a black silk shirt, canary sneakers and a multi-colored necklace. On my way to the bathroom, I get a glance of her whizzing by, keeping pace with Jordan's frequent back and forth running. She's almost moving fast enough to make those colors blend to white. Between sprints, Jordan stops and looks at Michelle out of the corner of his eye, making a low-pitched humming noise which Michelle is quick to repeat. As the Kaufmans had suggested to us, we in turn suggested to our helpers that imitating Jordan's actions might be a good way of getting his attention. So during times when we aren't initiating activities, we are typically imitating him. Michelle, even more than the others, seems to prefer this technique and employs it a lot.

She seems so happy in what she's doing that I'd like to take more time to observe her, but another high school student—Theresa—will be replacing her in forty-five minutes, and I want to take over with Jordan for a short while between their sessions so they can talk to each other about the program when Theresa arrives.

After a quick shower, I throw together dinner for Jordan and offer Michelle a fifteen-minute break if she'll stay and discuss her session with Theresa. I then enter the room carrying Jordan's dinner. "Put it on the table," he blurts out when he sees the food. It's a remark he's been making four times a day (during meal times and his snack) for over two weeks. He doesn't seem to really care where I put the food since he darts away from me the minute I'm in the room. Like so many of his most recent utterances, this habitual response seems more a ritual than an attempt at communication. It's spoken in a loud monotone with almost no emotion. Not only his speech, but nearly every aspect of his behavior has a canned quality about it these days, as if he were some living wind-up toy. Even the photographs from this period, when examined years later, would depict this programmed appearance, giving him the look of those life-sized cardboard figures of famous people with whom folks have their picture taken.

When Jordan gets finished with bouncing off the walls, he settles down to the dinner table for his meal. He sits quietly while I feed him, so I'm able to catch bits and pieces of Theresa and Michelle's conversation after Theresa arrives. They spend a minute or two talking about Jordan, but then a passing remark about a blouse metamorphoses into a discussion of mutual acquaintances, boys, and other stuff. It's the kind of "high school madness" talk I hadn't heard in nearly twenty years until we started this program.

While I shovel the food into Jordan's face, my mind drifts away from the discussion in the living room. One thought leads to another, and pretty soon I'm pondering what a strange life I have. Who else in the world, aside from drug dealers, has cars coming and going from his house all day? How many other fathers spend six hours a day playing with their sons in a little room? For that matter, how many parents have three-year-olds who are perfectly healthy and yet haven't seen the light of day for six weeks?

Time's up for reflection, though. Theresa is at the door waiting to do her session. Her presence in the room will present a marked contrast from the experience Jordan has had in the previous two hours. Whereas Michelle was a blur of color, motion, and sounds, Theresa is a quiet motherly type. Even in her most buoyant moments, she is barely audible from the living room. In spite of, or perhaps because of, her low-key approach, however, she is just as successful as any of us in getting Jordan's attention. And unlike the other high school kids, she is almost 100 percent reliable to show up for her sessions.

As he does on most occasions when another person enters the room, Jordan gets up from his chair when Theresa arrives. Since he's not finished his meal, I ask him if he wants any more to eat, to which he again replies, "Put it on the table." I point out that the food is already on the table, but he has turned his back on me by now, still saying, "Put it on the table."

Theresa smiles at this interaction. I let her know as I'm leaving that I intend to observe a little of her session. Not wanting to make her feel self-conscious, I explain that I just want to get ideas. But my concern on her behalf is unnecessary. Theresa is a very self-assured kid. In fact, she's almost oblivious to distractions when she is working with Jordan, and, for that reason, we use her as a model for a couple other volunteers.

Today Jordan is allowing her to approach him without bolting. He looks up at her and maintains eye contact for about three seconds, which Theresa is quick to notice and respond to with the pat phrase that we have been using on such occasions: "Good looking, Jordan!" Not long after the eye contact, Jordan hollers from the corner, "Daddy get on the floor!" A little bit surprised by this, Theresa turns around to see if I'm within Jordan's sight. Seeing that I'm not, she replies, "Daddy isn't here now, Jordan. Do you want me to get on the floor?" "Daddy get on the floor," he responds. "Here, I'll get on the floor," Theresa finally suggests, which seems to satisfy Jordan just as well. He doesn't care who provides the back, he just wants someone to sit or stand on.

This exchange, and the "Put it on the table" incident, reveal a troubling change in Jordan's use of language. Since his diagnosis, he had heretofore maintained, and to some extent even improved, his ability to communicate. True, his pattern represented stagnation more than development during this critical period for language growth: but there had never before been actual regression. In this new phase, however, he begins to use these over-specific phrases to convey a variety of messages. A saying such as "Put it on the table," for example, might be used to communicate "Leave the food here," or "Bring the food in," or "I'm ready to eat."

Other ominous signs emerge during the late winter to early spring period as well. Over the fifteen-month period we had known about his autism, we had labored assiduously to ensure that Jordan maintained the several hundred words that he had learned prior to the diagnosis. We also worked hard to help him learn new concepts such as prepositional phrases and spatial relationships. But all of that was accomplished under a philosophy which gave us the license to offer rewards or to cajole in order to get language. In our current mindset, however, we have decided to let Jordan choose when and how he will communicate. We still ask questions in the hope that he will respond, but language development per se is not the focus of our efforts during this regime. Now, over those many hours that I spend with him I begin to notice that both the frequency and the length of Jordan's utterances have begun to decrease. I am also concerned that he may have forgotten many of the words and concepts he had learned. But, at this point, there is no way of knowing whether he is unable or unwilling to participate in my attempts to have him use language. My frame of reference tends toward the pessimistic on this day when almost nothing that I or the others have done with him has elicited a favorable response.

It is nearly dinner time when I leave the hallway where I have been watching Theresa work with Jordan. I am exhausted and grateful that I don't have to do another session with Jordan today. Shortly, my sister-in-law, Kathy, will arrive to take over for Theresa, and when Jill comes home we have planned to eat out, so now seems a good time to do some planting in the garden. I wander down to the patch that I was so happy to turn over the first full growing season that we lived here. The ground seems so barren in this early spring season. It hasn't even been properly turned over; only the small row where I have intended to plant the spinach I'm about to put in the ground has been prepped.

It's a nice enough day to set a hoe scraping across soft dirt—the kind of day that would have sent me time traveling just a couple of years ago. Back then, I would no doubt have been comparing my good fortune with periods past, when such a life as I had come to know would have been unthinkable. Yes, there was once a wellspring of joy on this land. Something else is about to spring from me now.

Out of the corner of my moistening eye, I catch a glimpse of Kathy coming down the hill to the garden. Thankfully, I have enough time to pull myself together before I am discovered. One of the cardinal rules of the option program is to be happy, and I'm not about to spread a dispiriting attitude to any of the folks who are working with Jordan, especially Kathy or Jim, both of whom have worked so hard with us and given of themselves so unselfishly. "Craig, you even find time to get the garden in," Kathy says teasingly as she approaches. "Yes, and as you can see, this beautifully prepared patch should yield crops worthy of display at this year's county fair," I reply in mock pride.

After some polite chitchat, Kathy gets around to the reason she has arrived early. She has not felt that Jordan has been responding particularly well to her of late, and she's wondering if I have any suggestions. Unlike some others who might be working through their frustrations, Kathy is an especially forthright person who, perhaps because she has spent much of her young adult life around small children, is willing to say what's on her mind. I can tell by the way she presents the issue that she might even suspect that I am feeling the same way.

Wanting to be honest without discouraging her, I hesitantly reply, "Kath, I think we're all having a little difficulty reaching Jordan at this stage of the program. I don't have to tell you that there isn't much evidence yet that doing this thing is helping Jordan. All I can say is, do the best you can. We haven't been doing this very long, and maybe it will take time to win Jordan's trust." I wonder as I speak whether the lack of confidence I'm feeling has come across in my tone of voice. But Kathy seems to have anticipated my response. Nothing in her face shows marked dissatisfaction with my weak answer, and, after a little more polite conversation she's on her way to do her session.

Later that evening, after Jill and I have returned from dinner, I am sitting on the edge of the bed looking at a book, while Jill puts Jordan down for the night. The house is finally quiet, save for the gentle spring zephyr blowing through the maple tree directly outside our bedroom window. Beside me is the disordered heap of my avocation, the first three chapters of my dissertation. The book I'm examining in this leisure time is a text on research design, a tome whose information I remember only dimly from my initial exposure to it nearly five years ago. As I flip through the pages to find the appropriate statistical test for my study, I am asking myself those questions which must go through the minds of hundreds of doctoral candidates every year: "What is the point of this? Who will read this document when it's completed? What contribution does participating in this exercise make to my professional competence?"

While pondering these weighty questions, I notice that a folder I need has been placed under some other materials on the bookshelf. When I liberate it from the pile, a small book falls to the floor. I reach down to retrieve it, and get a visceral reaction as my hand makes contact with the book. It's the diary of Jordan's first years, and it is almost unbearable to touch. Like Superman's kryptonite, or Dracula's cross, the diary has acquired a power to transfigure me, to drain me of my energy, to render me terrified and disoriented. If I open it and turn to any page, I'll come face to face with the expression of a joy that I'm likely never to know again. I'll read of the exploits of a child who doesn't live here anymore. I'll be reminded of a time that has vanished. No, I'll hide this dangerous object under a big pile of papers. I won't allow it to make a casual entrance into my life again.

Now the phone is ringing, and I leap to answer it, not wanting the ring to disturb Jill's efforts to get Jordan to sleep. It's my mother calling with her weekly medical report on my father's condition. It's something she's been doing since the night we returned from the Option Institute, when she called to inform us that Dad had been placed in intensive care because his lungs had become essentially inoperative. Throughout the two-month period since, she has faithfully checked in with these updates. Tonight the news is good: Dad is gradually being weaned away from the machines that breathe for him. No word yet as to when he'll be out of the hospital, but the doctors are optimistic. As Mom relates this, I realize that I no longer believe that he'll recover. How can a person who has damaged his lungs, throat, and mouth to the extent that my father has, and who has undergone so many major medical interventions, come back from all of that? I need to go see him. In a month the baby will be here: maybe I can visit him shortly after that.

Now Jill emerges from Jordan's room. She drags her tired and increasingly heavy body toward the bed. "If there's a God in heaven, he'll stay asleep," she whispers as she settles down next to me. The wind picks up a notch and brings a chill to the room. We hunker down for a long night. Within three weeks my father would die suddenly from complications associated with his bout with cancer. I would never so much as speak to him during the time that he'd spend in the hospital. Nine days after his death, my daughter would arrive in the world to replace him. ❄

❄

❄

❄

❄ Even from the beginning, our participation in the Option program illustrates the dichotomy that lies in my soul as I confront the reality of Jordan. On the one hand, there is the memory of the vital, engaging toddler who spoke and laughed spontaneously, the child whose specter reemerges time and again over the eight-month period in which we maintain the program, leading me on a furious chase around his room in the

belief that if I would but say the right word or do the right
thing, he would reform from the ashes and take flight.

It is this spirit that prompts me, and Jill even more so, to
read beyond the text written for our eyes to the lines meant
only for the heart. Throughout that winter we tell ourselves
that he is becoming more social, or that his eye contact is increasing, or that he is more tuned in to his surroundings. Out
of these almost invisible threads we proceed to weave the
cloth of recovery. And too, we feed off the enthusiasm of our
helpers; always mistaking their exhilaration for the process as
tangible evidence of improvement in the product. Add to all
this the fact that there are times when he does seem to
respond to what we are doing, times when he indeed appears
to reach out to us, times when he actually graces our efforts
with a kind of primitive appreciation; and our faith in the
process is almost inevitable.

But the other element in my psyche refuses to overlook
Jordan's regression in language, cognitive, and social skills,
and persists in raising the point that belief in something must
sooner or later be rewarded with evidence that that something
works. After several months with only periods of fleeting
awareness to show for our efforts, some of the luster starts to
fade. The questions which we earlier raised about the core assumptions of this method now become serious doubts. The notion that Jordan could sense our attitudes when we were with
him, for example, seemed at least possible when we heard it at
the Option Institute, but as I try to assess my own and others'
attitudes over many sessions with Jordan, he doesn't appear to
differentiate his behavior according to any patterns that I can
surmise. And the belief that the bigger the action the more
likely that Jordan will respond to it doesn't seem to hold
either. In fact, he appears to try harder to evade the loud or
flashy gesture, displaying a look of anxiety when the person ap-

proaching him gets too close. And as disconcerting as these realizations are, they are not nearly as upsetting as our growing sense that the basic tenet of the Option method—that autistic children respond more normally when they are free to reject an activity or overture—doesn't seem to apply in Jordan's case.

Almost imperceptibly, the tough, disciplined edge of our efforts begins to soften about the time my father dies. An amalgam of factors that might not have been decisive in isolation, when brought together brings us to a critical juncture in how we view what we're doing with Jordan. The change of seasons is one such factor. In the winter it was easy to keep Jordan indoors all day and not feel as if he was missing much. But as the blossoms come out on the trees, and the mercury climbs, it seems almost cruel to confine him to a ten-by-twelve room. We wrestle with this feeling even though our mentors were adamant about keeping Jordan inside. It's a difficult call: Introducing him to the great outdoors at this point might undermine the whole program, but it might just as well invigorate our efforts. In ongoing conversations with another family who are doing a similar program with their child, we learn that they take him out frequently with no apparent ill effects. By the end of April we decide to do the same. At first our excursions are limited to a nearby playground, but before long Jordan is visiting relatives, going to restaurants, and even making an occasional trip to "play" with a child for whom one of our workers babysits.

Another event which weakens our resolve is the birth of our daughter, Leslie. Not only are we dealing with another child who requires full-time care, we're also concerned that running this type of program might be an inordinate strain on the development of one or both of the children. I'm particularly worried about Leslie's safety, now that we are letting Jordan have a somewhat freer run of the house. On one occasion Jordan actually steps on her after bolting from his room into the living room. No serious damage is done, but the incident leaves a lasting impression of the potential for scarier scenarios.

The improving weather and our expanded family aside, we have logistical and internal problems in our program as well. We learn the hard way that high school students can be unreliable, and that volunteers may feel free to cancel a session on very short notice, often leaving us in the position of having to do as much as five hours straight with Jordan. But even more troubling than the fatigue and disappointment inherent in doing double or triple sessions, is the sense that we're getting from our conversations with the various people working with us that they are feeling ineffective and rudderless. Despite some halting efforts initially, we have never been able to develop an esprit de corps among our staff. We don't have group meetings, and we make only cursory efforts at providing for sharing among the various participants, so there occurs only limited dialogue about the program, most of it transpiring between the others and us. And without this group camaraderie, it becomes an exacting task to keep everyone's spirits high.

Even with its associated tribulations, however, our resolve to stay with some form of an Option program for Jordan is strong as spring winds down. There really isn't a choice—that is, until we learn of Kiyo Kitahara.

The way that we learn of this remarkable woman, and the story which evolves after we do, comes straight out of the genre "only in America." It begins even before we start our program with Jordan, with an article sent to us by our good friend Debra (she of the hors d'oeuvres from an earlier and happier New Year's eve). That article covered the story of

Anoja, a woman who had spent nearly six months and a considerable portion of her family's life savings learning from the Kaufmans. It contained a first-hand account of the Option method, as well as an interview with this woman, who was a native of Sri Lanka now living in a suburb of Washington, D.C. Reading the article played a small part in our final decision to go with the at-home approach, as this woman's enthusiasm for the Option method seemed genuine.

Months later, in the midst of our own Option program, we hear of her again from a young veterinarian from Virginia who has been studying with the Kaufmans, and who is interested in meeting families who are employing the Option Program with a handicapped child. During his visit with us, he mentions that he has been in contact with this woman, but that she never actually got a program off the ground due to an inability to find volunteers.

Since she isn't doing a program, we never think of calling Anoja until things begin to deteriorate at home. Wanting to know what option succeeded Option, however, Jill finally does decide to contact her in the middle of May. And when she does, what we learn is almost unbelievable. Her boy is now a student in a school in Japan. What's more, perhaps as many as twenty-five other American children with autism are also enrolled in the school, several of whom had earlier been involved in home programs like the one we are doing with Jordan. In fact, Anoja had herself learned about this extraordinary venture from a parent of a former Option "star."

The opportunity that this news presents is, above all, the chance to think anew. For over a year we have been telling ourselves that there are no educational solutions for Jordan, that only a medical breakthrough or a total commitment of love would return him to his earlier self. Like Humpty Dumpty, his fragile mental state had been so irreparable damaged in our view that mere king's horses and men would not be enough. It would take a sorcerer of some sort to bring him back, and even at this late date, we believe in his second coming.

Certainly, no school that we've ever seen or heard of came even close to fitting this bill. But maybe schools with which we are familiar don't work because they employ a faulty model. Perhaps if the philosophy of instruction were radically different, a more hopeful outcome could be achieved. At any rate, if the people at this school in Tokyo can convince American parents to leave their children on the other side of the globe, they seem worth investigating.

But how can we learn about the philosophy and methodology of a little-known school, from an entirely different culture, located halfway around the world? There are, of course, the parents of the children enrolled in the school, and Anoja has the telephone numbers of a few of these. But we want more than that: we want to be able to talk directly with the administrators and teachers of this school; we want to be able to see the children in action—both the Japanese children and the Americans enrolled in the international division of the operation; and we want to be able to examine a written account of the philosophy and methods of the school, in order that we might form an impression of how Jordan would do under this type of instruction. In less than two months we would have all of these.

IV

*A*fter a long, moonless night on the ocean of forgetful-
ness, your boat crashes on the shore in a land that is unfamiliar. This place where you have found yourself may be
mild or severe of climate; its soil could be fertile or unyielding;
its populace friendly or hostile. The circumstances of your condition are totally beyond your control—you have just been
born. I have these idle thoughts while holding my daughter,
not yet a month old, in the palm of my hand.

Gazing down at her tiny face, I get a sense of how much
her and Jordan's beginnings are alike, and also how much they
are dramatically different. Like Jordan she came into the
world in the time of azalea blossoms; like Jordan her face
defines beauty for her parents; and like Jordan she can know
nothing of what awaits her in this life. But there is a vast difference in the household into which Jordan arrived and that
which welcomes Leslie. At this moment of staring deeply into
my daughter's face, I believe I understand the meaning of this
experiential chasm—it is that I and, to a lesser extent, her
mother are without joy. Though, like most parents, we see our
new little daughter as a sweet, cuddly, good-natured infant
who evokes love and pride, we are unable to make this equation add up to the exhilaration which would be typical in this
situation. I wonder to myself as I relax, trying to let her control the ebb and flow of our interaction on this lovely spring
morning, whether a baby can pick up such a deficiency as the
absence of joy in her parents, and whether there is reason to
hope that this situation might change.

From out under the maple tree in the backyard, I hear Jill
hanging up the phone in our bedroom. Between humming
and cooing at Leslie, I was able to pick up bits and pieces of

her conversation with Dr. Kitahara's assistant, Katsumi Suzuki. Now Jill comes bounding out of the house to give me the details.

It seems that Dr. Kitahara will be in Boston in two weeks, making arrangements for the opening of her school in America. At that time she wants to see Jordan to determine whether he would be appropriate for her program. Now we'll have a chance to meet the teacher whose students wowed them at the autism society's convention with a stellar musical performance; the teacher whose students ride unicycles and do complicated gymnastics routines; the teacher who has suggested that by reducing an autistic child's anxiety and developing his fitness, one can expect significant improvement in behavior, functioning, and cognition.

But who is this woman? How did she develop these ideas? And how can we begin to assess the validity of her claims? Over the past few weeks we have been in contact with about ten parents of children enrolled in the International Division of Musashino Higashi Gakuen, all reporting high levels of satisfaction. One of the parents active in having the International Division moved to Boston is especially enthusiastic about the school. He tells us of plans to have a contingent of American educators and scientists visit Tokyo in order to render what he feels certain will be a favorable opinion regarding its operation. He has followed up his phone calls with a barrage of written information about the school, consisting mainly of newspaper and magazine articles. Additionally, our initial contacts with the staff at Musashino have enabled us to obtain copies of Dr. Kitahara's books.

What we have learned from our preliminary investigation is that Dr. Kitahara has been an educator of nondisabled children for over thirty years; that she has had her own school in which she has taught both normal and autistic children for twenty years; that she has developed her methods, called "Daily Life Therapy," largely by trial and error, in working with hundreds of autistic children, and that her program is radically different from anything being done in the West. Her methodology consists of three pillars: vigorous physical exercise, education in a group setting, and intense instruction in the visual and performing arts.

Having done less than a month's worth of homework, and never having seen any of Dr. Kitahara's students, it is difficult to get overly enthusiastic about her program. We have, after all, been to other states—and other states of mind—in search of answers to Jordan's problem. But even at this early date, there are elements of Daily Life Therapy that have an intuitive appeal. Take, for instance, vigorous physical exercise: over the course of the past six months, Jordan has had very little of it. And it seems that his muscle tone has deteriorated, while his problems falling asleep and staying asleep persist. According to Dr. Kitahara's theory, a daily period of aerobic exercise would contribute to normalized eating and sleeping patterns. It just makes sense; if exercise is important in the lives of normal people for reducing stress and producing a sense of well-being, how much more would it be so for an extremely hyper and anxious child?

The idea of group education, though radically different from anything we've tried educationally, also seems sensible to me. Over the period of time that we and others have been working with Jordan, the one-on-one method has been fairly consistently employed. And throughout that same period we have seen no long-term improvement. Indeed, recently there has been regression. Maybe Dr. Kitahara is correct in her assumption that so much individual attention only exacerbates the autistic child's already high level of anxiety. This would seem to be true in Jordan's case, where even varying his ability to control his participation in activities did not appear to help much. Perhaps he would relax sufficiently to be able to learn, not only from his teacher but from others, if he weren't receiving so much individual attention.

And the idea of intense instruction in the arts makes the most sense of all. Throughout his education, Jordan has never had anything resembling an organized curriculum which attempted to teach him how to do things. While we were working with him within the behavior modification framework, for example, the focus of our efforts was limited to vocabulary and concept development. During the time he spent in public school special education, he was exposed to a greater variety of activities, but there was little intensity or organization. And in his current situation, instruction has been abandoned altogether in favor of helping him relate better to others. Dr. Kitahara's belief that autistic children, like their normal counterparts, learn best by doing seems so obvious in retrospect that I feel ashamed that as an educator of young children I hadn't realized this sooner.

The warm spring morning of a few hours ago has slowly evolved into a humid, summer-like afternoon. Under the shade of the maple tree I feel the peaceful breathing of a sleeping daughter against my chest, and I realize that I am tired of chasing a miracle. I want to relax—to the extent that this is possible—and enjoy a natural relationship with my son. I want him to go to a school and be one among many children, not neglected, but neither subjected to frantic individual attention. But even in this moment of apprehension and gentle communion with my daughter, I am still unable to abandon my illusion that Jordan's autism is merely a trance, from which he will emerge if I and the others in our program only work hard enough. ❊

❊

❊

❊

❊ The plane touches down in Boston on a brilliantly sunny morning in the beginning of summer. Across the aisle Jill's fingers are relinquishing their rigor mortis grip on the arm rests of her chair as she realizes that we've safely returned to terra firma. Rising quickly from my seat to block Jordan's path as the plane unloads, I think what a stressful last couple of hours Jill has just spent. Not only has she been confined to the small space of an airplane seat with an autistic four-year-old, she has also had to fight her serious fear of flying. And we're just beginning our fun. Once we're out of the plane, we'll have to locate a taxi, negotiate our way through an unfamiliar city, and then find some way of keeping Jordan occupied in the lobby of a hotel for three hours; after which we'll have to reverse the steps.

Steps one and two of our post-flight ordeal actually go relatively smoothly, but waiting for three hours for our interview with Dr. Kitahara gets old pretty quickly. We spend the bulk of our time walking back and forth along the road that runs in front of the hotel. It's a fairly busy road that doesn't afford much time for reverie when it's being traversed with an active preschooler who hasn't been around a lot of traffic recently. But as I walk along this road across from the Charles River, I feel a tremendous affinity for the sufferer of the common cold. For here I am in the backyards of MIT and Harvard, hub of America's intellectual life, looking into the bright faces of the students and teachers as they jog, cycle, or row by. I feel an irresistible urge to call out, "Hey, you of the high-powered minds, why can't any of you explain to me why this child with no ostensible brain damage is regressing? How is it that you haven't developed a pill, or a machine, or a surgical or educational technique to help kids such as him?" But at that same time, I am aware that this disorder, like that nemesis, the common cold, is a Rubik's Cube of a mystery that will require the efforts of many minds over a period of many years to solve.

After the endless afternoon of time-killing, we finally get our interview with Dr. Kitahara. As we enter the little hotel room, she holds out her hands towards Jordan, beaming a soft smile reflective of inner peace. So taken does she seem with him, that she barely responds to our greeting, and even before we begin the discussion of our situation, she decides to have a private audience with him out in the hall. Thus she and the interpreter, Mr. Suzuki, leave, carrying Jordan along. On their way out, Mr. Suzuki lets us know that this session will probably be all Dr. Kitahara will need to determine whether Jordan will be appropriate for her program. When they return, about twenty minutes later, Dr. Kitahara's face gives away the answer to the question for which we have been waiting breathlessly—Jordan, in Mr. Suzuki's words, is Dr. Kitahara's "type."

The balance of the interview with Dr. Kitahara is taken up with questions about the opening of the new school and her impression of Jordan's potential. Although not all of the details have been ironed out, Dr. Kitahara exudes a determined self-assurance about everything being finalized before the start of the school year: Boston Higashi will open in September. And she's even more confident of what she can do for Jordan—confident enough to suggest that, if the school is unable to begin this year, we should not hesitate to enroll Jordan in Tokyo.

Sunset descends on the east coast as our plane retraces the route from Boston to Baltimore. The shadow of the Holy Grail seems to rise from the west in the wake of the departing sun, tempting us to follow; across a vast ocean, to another morning, in a different world. ❄

❄

❄

❄

❄ We aren't back in Maryland long before we are faced with the reality of making a monumental decision. In early July we learn that the Boston Higashi School will indeed be another year in opening. For the second time in less than a year, it's crunch time once again. But this is substantially different from our decision to begin an Option program; we're not just deciding whether to take leaves of absence from our jobs or to spend substantial sums of money; we're deciding whether or not to put our child in a school on the other side of the world. How can we ever be sufficiently confident that doing this will make a difference? ❄

❄

❄

❄

❄ Heisenberg's "uncertainty principle" reminds us that the more we know about one variable of a particle's behavior, the less we know about another. Specifically, the more we

know about a particle's position, the less we know about its
velocity. As a law of physics, this principle stands as a significant, but essentially undistinguished, member of a set of
equally important, if tentative, truths about the way the
universe functions. As a metaphor for the way one experiences life, however, it is unparalleled. Transferred to the macro
world of human endeavors, it tells us that the most we can
ever hope to know about a situation will always be defined by
the parameters of a probability statement. The various steps
along the path through Jordan's autism are testament to the
truth of this observation. In choosing behavior modification
as a starting point for his treatment, for example, we had
begun with a method that stood above the others in its docu-
mented success with autistic children. Probabilistically speaking, it was the best bet for a kid with Jordan's developmental
history. Yet, whether due to a flaw in technique, or attitude,
or some internal condition specific to Jordan, the approach
failed. When an educational solution didn't offer much help,
the odds suggested that a higher functioning kid like Jordan
would likely benefit from some kind of drug treatment. But
that, too, proved to be a Chimera. And when the drugs failed,
following a method which emphasized motivation and
Jordan's ability to control his surroundings seemed, even in
retrospect, to have been the next best choice.

But the universe is only probabilistic, not exact. And in
this summer, when my child, who—according to everyone's
probability statement—was supposed to improve has instead
done the reverse, I realize that I know very little about any of
the variables affecting him. And in running to the various
solutions to his mystery, I have become like the man who lost
his wallet in a dark part of town, but insisted on looking for it
under street lamps because that's where the light was best.

By the middle of August, 1986, Jordan has almost no spontaneous speech. He responds only to the most insistent commands. His contact with people is minimal. His mood is generally sour, except on those occasions when he is allowed to be totally by himself, or is given foods he likes such as fruits, bread, and sweets. Our time is short—less than three weeks. Based on no first-hand knowledge, and very little second-hand information, we must resolve to stick with a program that is failing, go back to a program that failed, or place our child in a program where we would have almost no access to him. God provides you with the dilemma; it's up to you to find Solomon.

The air is jungle wet and still, not the kind of day meant for a temper tantrum. But if you're four and frustrated and losing your mind, the weather is not much of a deterrent. Just back from a trip with Theresa to his "friend" Vincent's, Jordan apparently didn't get enough of a car ride home; or maybe he thought he was supposed to stop off at the local McDonald's for a coke; or maybe he was expecting better company than his father when he got home. Whatever the reason, he is clearly unhappy. He lies on the ground, banging his fists and crying. I am clearly unable to meet his needs. Since we are theoretically still doing an Option program, I play along with the scene and alternate between imitating him and trying to amuse him out of his mood, with neither approach having any effect.

I am not sure whether it would be attributed to fatigue from prolonged exposure to stress, or to simple depression, or to the growing realization that my mind is already made up about leaving Jordan in Japan, but I am less emotionally in-volved with his frequent outbursts these days. Four or five times a day, for up to twenty minutes at a time, he enters these rage states, either spinning violently or lying down and screaming. And when he does, I seem likely as not to enter my own state—a dreamy kind of out-of-body detachment that minimizes my connection with the event. But this feeling is not just limited to times when he is unhappy. On walks, at meal times, and even when playing with him I can slip into this mind-set in which his presence no longer can evoke a visceral reaction within me. It is as if a subliminal message has been planted in my brain, reminding me that soon, he will be living in a dormitory in a foreign country; a resident of Japan on a student visa—at the age of four. Increasingly, I experience life in the manner of a certain tribe of Malaysian natives who believe that dreams are more fundamental than reality.

Jordan is finished with his tantrum, and Jill has completed her conversation with Theresa about his afternoon with Vincent. It's the worst hour of the day—4 in the afternoon; the time when Jordan is crankiest; the time when he's looking for something to eat but it's too early for dinner. Jill is tired and needs to relax and to nurse Leslie, so it's up to me to come up with entertainment. I choose swimming for its ability to give Jordan a workout without us both having to suffer through the day's unbearable humidity. Having spent part of the summer reading Dr. Kitahara's books, we have seen the benefits of a structured exercise period even before Jordan is enrolled in the school. Our only problem has been in getting him to participate in these activities. Water play, however, is one form of exercise that we can structure to a limited degree, and it has the added advantage of being an activity that Jordan seems to enjoy.

After a few minutes in the car, Jordan is back to the demilitarized zone. He silently gazes out the window at the rush hour traffic as we travel along Baltimore's Beltway en route to the college pool. This is his home—the car. He can sit back and be transported, maybe to another consciousness, without having to worry about anyone trying to get his attention to ask, tell, or show him something. It is the only place over the past two years where he has seemed consistently at ease. And it is the only device in our environment that has provided us with any meaningful respite throughout his autistic period.

It's always a bit tricky when the dream machine stops, though. We can never be sure that Jordan will happily disembark at the destination. Today, fortunately, he's pleased with the arrangement. He recognizes that we're in the parking lot of his favorite playground and considers that he's about to be given license to splash. Upon entering the building, we pass the desk of the young manager of the phys-ed complex. He knows Jordan and is aware of his peculiar behavior, so he doesn't get too unnerved when Jordan runs headlong into a hotly contested basketball game in the middle of a fast break. The interruption of play, which is prolonged by the zigzag chase that ensues, does not appear to be viewed as a cute diversion by the game's participants, however. But Jordan is finally corralled, and play quickly resumes as I slink into the locker room, thinking that Jordan is getting old enough to stand out as strange.

As we change into swimsuits, Jordan is a whirling dervish of excitement. He knows just where he is and what is about to take place. He also knows how to get to the pool from the locker room, where the bathroom is, where we put our towels when we enter the pool, and every other aspect of the routine. What's more, he follows directions and maintains a demeanor throughout the swimming period that is little suggestive of autism. In almost every other public place, I feel compelled to offer explanations for his unusual behavior, but here at the pool, I rarely have to apologize, for he just seems like any active, focused, and happy preschooler.

Today there's an added bonus to our experience—the water is perfect. Together Jordan and I slide off the edge and into the water. As usual, I begin our water play by tossing him up in the air and catching him as he hits the surface of the water. After he tires of this, I drag him along the top of the water and do various rough house stuff until he looks like he just wants to hold on to the side. During the past few weeks I have been trying to get Jordan to kick off the side and swim to my outstretched hands at this point in the routine. But he's been a little timid and has, heretofore, required that my hand be within a very short distance of his. Today, though, without any prompting, he shoves right off from the side and paddles the five feet that separates us as if he'd been doing it all his life. Immediately upon completing this feat, he lets out with a squeal that sounds so normal, so unlike any sound that he has made recently that I have to look twice at him to make sure that I haven't picked up another kid. I, too, make an unusual sound that could be characterized as a cross between a cheer and a cry. "Jordan, you're swimming! You did it! Look, let's swim further." I move about twelve feet from the side after I deposit him on the ledge and beckon him to repeat the act, which he does with glee. Again and again he goes back to the wall and then back to me, each time squealing as if it was the first time he had ever experienced the feeling of competence, or freedom, or bliss. That night would be the last time he'd sleep through the night during his final days at home. ❄

❄

❄

❄

❋ It is September 1, 1986, one day short of the forty-first anniversary of V.J. Day. On that day in 1945, the Japanese emperor was probably en route to the ship where he would sign the unconditional surrender ending the war. Not very far from that spot, my father was aboard a ship awaiting news of the birth of his first child; an event which would occur only nine days later. Today, in 1986, Jill and I are about to sign our own surrender in Japan—the surrender of our only son. We have battled his autism for twenty-one months to the day, and though we have employed the most modern of weaponry, we have failed. It is another irony of life that Schopenhauer might have appreciated, that the offspring of a people who might easily have killed my father are now being asked to save my son.

We have a suitcase full of clothes with labels sewn in them, we have an ample supply of Benadryl, we have babysitting coverage for Leslie and a ride to the airport. What we don't have is our sanity. For even if you have considerable evidence that your child is hopelessly regressing; even if there is reason to believe that where you are taking him is probably better for him than where he is; even if what you're doing is certainly better for the other members of the family; it is impossible to escape the magnitude of this action—leaving your four-year-old in the care of strangers in another country.

Our friend Dave pulls up in his wagon ready for the trip to Washington's National Airport. My mother, who is taking the initial shift with Leslie, hugs her grandson goodbye, knowing she probably won't get to do it again until Jordan has turned five. And Jill and I are at each other's throats over some minor details of the trip, no doubt arising from the immense burden of the decision we are about to make.

Our anxiety-based anger subsides once we're in the car and on our way. The trip to the airport and the preliminary arrangements once there go smoothly. We have enough time to check our bags, confirm our seat assignments, take Jordan to the bathroom and walk around the terminal before we have to board. We also get an unexpected break after we board: because the plane isn't full and because we've let the flight attendants know that Jordan has autism, they are letting us sit in business class. We'll have a little more room to maneuver, which should make things go a bit easier.

The reality of what a fifteen-hour plane ride with an autistic child is going to be like doesn't take too long to set in, though. We're not even off the ground before he's expressing serious displeasure about being aboard the airplane. He alternates between squirming out of his seat and into the aisle and knocking his head and back against the chair. In the midst of the tempest, one of our fellow travellers turns to us and relates the hope that Jordan won't be doing this the entire trip. Obviously concerned that this might just be the case, Jill replies in an affected niceness, "Lady, if this is all the worse he behaves, we'll be lucky."

Once, as a child, I dreamed of living in a place where it was always day time. On this plane trip I get to experience the horror of what that might be like. We depart from Washington around 9:30 a.m. and ride with the sun halfway around the world. No matter how many window shades are pulled, it never gets dark. No matter how hard we try, we can't get comfortable, nor are we able to sleep. And, no matter what we do, we can't help Jordan to settle down. Even with heavy sedation, he sleeps less than two hours during the entire trip.

All "day" long we are busy, taking turns trying to keep Jordan reasonably happy. We feed him favorite foods, we point out the sights from the window, we walk him from the front to the back of the plane—maybe thirty times. But mostly he is

restless and unhappy. It is a true hell for him—confinement
with all of these people—and there's no way he'll relax. When
the interminable ride is finally over, we still have an hour of
airport time, getting the baggage and going through customs.
And the crowd and confusion of Tokyo's airport is enough to
send a normal adult over the edge, so one can only imagine
what it must be doing to this autistic four-year-old who has
had less than two hours sleep in the last twenty-one hours.
After we have cleared customs, we struggle with our heavy
bags to the rendezvous point. For a while no one shows up,
and we worry that some miscommunication has occurred. But,
finally, a pleasant fellow steps out from the throng and asks if
we're the Schulzes. What a relief! Here's a person who can
take us away from this madness to a place where we can rest.
It's late afternoon in Tokyo: maybe we'll get to the school in
time to get something to eat and put Jordan to bed. Tomorrow
will be a busy day for him. He'll be handed over to someone
else's care. It would be nice if he could spend a restful final
evening with us.

Our contact, Mr. Matsumoto, leads us to the van which
will take us to Musashino, the Tokyo suburb where the school
is located. It's maybe forty miles from the airport, so we estimate that the trip will take an hour. To our amazement and
chagrin, Mr. Matsumoto suggests it might take a little longer,
say about an hour and a half longer. And his estimate proves
about right. It is in fact almost 7:00 when we arrive at the
school, and despite his lack of sleep on the plane, Jordan has
remained hyperactive throughout the crawl through the
crammed streets of Tokyo. Even when we arrive at the school
he doesn't fall asleep. The entire night he sleeps for maybe
three hours, squeezed between jumping off the bed and banging on the walls.

Finally, the sun rises on the first day of school in Tokyo. At nine o'clock we are to meet with Dr. Kitahara and the kindergarten teacher; following which Jordan will go off to his class, and we'll be given a tour of Musashino's various campuses. During the four-hour period since he has been awake, we have tried to keep Jordan busy with walks, a bath, and snacking on the bread and juices which are available in the room adjacent to our bedroom. The time drags such that the past thirty-six hours have seemed like thirty-six days, but eventually Dr. Kitahara and Ms. Shimizu arrive, coming into the snacking room in the middle of our third breakfast.

Jordan's initial contact with his new teacher is not propitious. As she approaches him with an enthusiastic greeting, he empties the contents of his mouth on her shirt.

Ms. Shimizu is undaunted, however: her smile seems to beam right through him as she extends a jubilant invitation for Jordan to have fun with her in the kindergarten.

Right away I like this teacher. I am reassured that she's in control and am pleasantly surprised by her facility with English. The way she strides off with Jordan gives me confidence, not only in her, but in this school as well. And this affecting beginning is just the first in a series of impressive experiences that day. After leaving the administrative building, we visit the vocational facility, the elementary and junior high campuses, and the kindergarten, all of which have mixed student bodies, with about one-quarter to one-third of the students having autism, and the rest nondisabled. At each site Dr. Kitahara addresses rows of eager, shining faces at opening day ceremonies, going out of her way to introduce us and another set of American parents to the students. At each site we see and even talk to autistic children who are being mainstreamed in spite of their handicaps. And at each site we witness highly structured lessons delivered by enthusiastic teachers to motivated and attentive students. As the day progresses, Jill and I become increasingly confident that having Jordan attend a Japanese school might not be as crazy as it seems.

After several more days of observing Jordan working in his class and meeting with the Musashino staff, we are in agreement that "Daily Life Therapy" represents our best option. We sign the unconditional surrender—a personal check for the first half of the school year.

On the final day of our stay, Jill and I rise early to jog. The narrow streets of Musashino are almost empty as we pass the huge apartment buildings with their balconies full of drying laundry, the large garden plots, and the small shops. Occasionally a bike, motorcycle, or tiny Japanese truck passes by to break the rhythmic patter of our feet. By the time we've finished, the streets are coming alive. While Jill showers, I take a short walk to cool down, making a mental movie of Jordan's future surroundings to take home with me. Japanese children in uniforms walk by in groups on their way to school. They are chatting with each other, but not in the way I'm used to hearing elementary school children talk. I can barely hear them. So young to be so quiet, I think.

When we leave for the airport, the driver swings by the school. Jordan and his classmates are on the playground. He looks lost and confused—almost frozen at the top of the slide—as some Japanese classmates urge him to go down. "Go down, Jordan," I encourage along in my head. "Good-bye, little boy. See you at Christmas." The urge to touch him one last time is almost overwhelming. A knot that feels like a golf ball

forms in my throat. As the car pulls away from the
playground, Jill clamps down on my arm and cries silently. ❄

❄

❄

❄

  ❄ It's here! I snatch the package out of the mailbox and
tear it open, leaving dropped mail on the ground as I fumble
my way into the house. This video postcard that I'm about to
watch is the first view we've had of Jordan in nearly four
weeks. During the time we've been out of touch, it seems that
we have thought only of him. At night as we got ready for
bed, we would think out loud about how he was now in
school. At breakfast we would comment that he was about to
go to bed. The sun never set on our thoughts of him. Now we
would be able to see what at least a few minutes of his life over
that period had been like.
  My fingers fly to get the tape into the machine and roll-
ing. It seems to take forever to get to the footage of Jordan,
but at last his face appears. He is on a walk with his teachers
and classmates through the little park adjacent to the kindergarten. Melancholy piano music plays in the background, ac-
centuating the sadness his face exudes, a sadness that
resonates tremendously with my own as my eyes follow his
vacant motion across the screen.
  From the park to the school to the scene at the dormitory
his lugubrious expression seems to follow him no matter what
the activity. It is difficult to watch this tape without second
guessing the wisdom of what we've done, without aching to
give him some comfort. On the other hand, if you take his
mood out of the equation, there is much about this video that

is positive. The fact that he is walking calmly, holding someone's hand; that he's eating a variety of foods; that he is sitting in a classroom paying attention to a teacher; this is all new and encouraging.

That evening Jill and I sit and watch the tape over and over. Though she is clearly as concerned as I am about Jordan's apparent unhappiness, Jill, too, feels that what we are seeing represents progress. There is no denying that Jordan's cooperativeness and attention span have improved. And others with less emotional involvement than we, when viewing the tape later, would make many of the same observations. No need to book another flight to Tokyo yet.

Between the viewing of this tape and the arrival of the next in early November, my thoughts of Jordan drop off dramatically. Up until the time that the first tape arrived, I was still in the grips of the adrenalin flow that drove us through the Option program. Now, as if transported to a place that has just been visited with a natural disaster, I move like a dazed survivor among the rubble. There seems almost no energy left to devote to my career or to prepare for the defense of my dissertation just a month away.

Around the house I listlessly peruse notes and anticipate my presentation. I can't help thinking of those discussions from introductory Psychology classes about the relationship between anxiety levels and test performance. As I recall, high levels of anxiety negatively affected performance, and moderate levels enhanced it. But what if your anxiety level was zero? Even less than a week before the orals I'm spending much more time raking leaves than studying: and this despite the fact that I have a tough committee who'll ask pointed questions, posing great potential, not only for failure, but for making me look utterly foolish.

On the fateful day of the defense, my performance nearly exceeds my wildest nightmares. There are questions to which I have no response, questions for which my answers seem absurd even as I give them, and questions to which I respond with statements in clear contradiction to the text of my paper. On top of that, I don't show the common sense to exhibit some anxiety or remorse. After being excused from the room, I calmly take a short walk around the building, a sufficient time, I think, for the committee to soundly reject my application for admission to the club. I try to formulate an apology for my advisor, who has shown great patience in steering me through an exercise that I've been less than diligent in completing.

After somewhat more time than I'd anticipated, my advisor leads the rest of the committee out of the room. She is smiling; I have passed. I am to suffer the fate disdained by Groucho Marx—being admitted to that club that I would prefer not joining because it would have me as a member. Each of the committee members passes by briskly, offering congratulations on their way to some more important business—like dinner.

No celebratory atmosphere awaits me at home, though a slew of my in-laws are present when I get there. Everyone is too busy watching the latest tape from Tokyo, which arrived earlier in the week. The now "Dr. Schulze" takes his place on the living room floor for his twentieth viewing of "Jordan: A Life in Tokyo, Chapter II." Everyone in attendance agrees that this second tape has a great deal more positive about it than the first. For starters, Jordan isn't continuously morose. And in many parts of the film he is even interacting positively with his teachers. Here he is touching the face of Ms. Shimizu, there he grins at Mr. Takamatsu after the latter has swung him around by the arms. He seems to be establishing relationships with the people in this program well beyond those which he'd formed with the people in the public school or the at-home programs. And this pattern that we began to notice on the second tape would extend throughout the year, with many of the tapes showing Jordan approaching his teachers to be tickled, or swung, or simply to get attention. What we don't see—language—we believe will come again in time, especially since he appears to understand the things being said to him.

With Jordan gone, and the work for the dissertation finished, my life reverts to a pattern similar to that which characterized Jordan's early days. There are no immediate issues to attend to, so Jill and I can begin to recover from the holocaust of the past two years. But though we are free from the relentless pressures of life with an autistic child, we have two major long-term fears to deal with. First, we must figure out how we will continue to pay a minimum of $25,000 a year for Jordan's education, since we don't foresee public assistance forthcoming for such an unorthodox school. And second, we must contend with our ongoing concerns about Leslie.

All kinds of scenarios seem possible with regard to the first of our problems. Even though Dr. Kitahara has expressed the belief that Jordan could return to a public school setting after three years at Higashi, neither of us thinks that this is likely. The reality is that Jordan is nonverbal and socially dysfunctional. Daily Life Therapy may hold many wonderful things for him, but it doesn't seem as if it could possibly turn him around that fast. We must consider, too, that even though the $25,000 price tag is beyond the cost of a Harvard education in 1986, it is immensely cheaper than most residential facilities handling children with autism; therefore, the cost can only go up. We are lucky: we have saved enough money to carry us through a few years of this kind of expense.

But what awaits us beyond that point? Jill reminds me to live day to day.

The second problem is, of course, a lot scarier, especially since Leslie seems to behave very much like Jordan did as a sixteen-month-old. We look for signs every day that might differentiate her from him, but nothing that she does certifies her as normal. Relatives speak to us of the look in her eyes, of her cued-in social response, of her affectionate nature; and I reply to their confidence with memories of a baby I knew to have all of these. And if Leslie were to be autistic, what then? In the privacy of our bedroom, in the cover of night, we think the unmentionable.

Almost four months pass before either Jill or I get to see Jordan. Soon after enrolling him in the school, we decided that each of us would visit him once during the year. I would go during the Christmas vacation and Jill would visit during the school's February "Year End Celebration," a time that the children from Musashino's various campuses put on special performances for parents.

Two days after Christmas I'm boarding another plane for my second trip to Tokyo.

December 29, 1986 (Tokyo)

After an almost inedible breakfast at a local restaurant, it was off to see the boy. Alas, life is not without screams. When I arrived at the administration building, I was greeted by Suzuki and Dr. Kitahara, and spent about half an hour talking with them about matters related to the opening of the school next year. And when I did finally get to the dorm, as might be expected, Jordan was sick.

He did recognize me when he saw me, though, and gave me some of those old head bumping kisses. But he was clearly not well and seemed pretty agitated. The lady taking care of him suggested that we let him join the other children upstairs in the playroom. Here, Jordan seemed more like his old self, jumping and acting hyper and avoiding me and everyone else. Though he did participate in the organized group dancing, he seemed really out of it, until the kids were taken to the cafeteria for a snack. He wasn't too sick or unfocused to eat his ice cream. Looking like the Jordan of old, in fact, he gobbled it up.

After this, the kids were treated to a Jiminy Cricket video which didn't get anybody's attention. Following the show, there was general agreement by everyone involved that I shouldn't take Jordan back to the hotel today. They suggested that he rest at the dorm in the afternoon and that I visit with him at dinner later that evening.

December 31, 1986

An almost full day with Jordan. Tanaka (the dormitory chief) brought him to the hotel around 10:00 this morning with a bag full of clothes. Unfortunately, he had his persistent cold, so we decided to scrap the plan to take him swimming in favor of a day of walks around the area and a train trip to a park suggested by the hotel clerk.

Jordan's behavior was a good bit like it had been four months earlier, with two noticeable exceptions. First, he never said any words—not even to request food. Second, he showed somewhat greater interest in objects. He really seemed to like the musical toy he received as a Christmas gift from his grandmother. He made it produce sounds about twenty times. He also liked the bear he was given by his other grandparents, carrying it to dinner and touching it several times.

All things considered, the day went better than I had expected, particularly taking into account Jordan's cold, and the fact that we had to spend most of the time in the tiny hotel room. On our walks and during the train ride, Jordan didn't balk too much, and he was willing to hold my hand most of the time. At the park though, he was definitely agitated and wouldn't go down the slide or play on the other equipment and on two occasions knocked down other kids, leaving me at a little bit of a loss to undo

our "ugly American" image, not knowing the Japanese
word for "autistic."

January 1, 1987

At the dorm they were unable to locate a bathing suit
for Jordan, so I was forced to change my plans for the
daily outing. It was an annoying surprise that got me off
on the wrong foot, since the weather was quite cold and
there was little to do at the hotel. Aside from a brief walk
to find Jordan some vaseline for his chapped nose, and an
aborted outing to the park—he wet his pants as we got off
the train—we wound up spending the entire day in the
room and hallway of the hotel.

It amounted to a 6-hour "session," though I was
more relaxed about his behavior and tried to observe him
to determine what, if anything, caught his attention. The
pattern of the past two days continued. He handled
several objects and semi-examined them. He made several
nonverbal requests, such as going to the door and pulling
me along, and bringing me a jar of peanut butter, clearly
indicating a desire to have it opened. He also sat beside me
for a few minutes and watched a soccer match on
television. And he once looked up at me and smiled when
we were running on the way to the train station.

His language is definitely becoming a problem. It may
be that the expressive language center has atrophied. He
was unwilling or unable to produce any words, but did
make a cow's "moo" as an attempt to say "more" for
more juice. His receptive language—at least for following
commands—is still intact. He understood phrases such as
"hold my hand," "put it on the bed," "take your shoes
off," and many others.

January 2, 1987

When we ask for a little meaning to things, the world
is so silent. I'm too big to be crying in this airport.

It was very good to see and be with Jordan this morning: and, for a change, the dorm staff was understanding.
They gave me the big playroom upstairs to spend my last

hour and a half with him. At first he seemed bothered that
he had to be with me, but I was able to make friends with
him by talking gently and by letting him take sips from the
bottle of juice I'd gotten for him on the way to the dorm.
(He has been drinking amazing quantities of liquid since
I've been with him—five bottles of grape and orange juice
and the better part of two cokes, as well as several glasses
of water, yesterday).

Periodically, he would come over and get the juice
and then fly away. But I kept a steady stream of quiet
prattle going, and eventually he seemed to come to trust
me. At least three times he looked at me for periods longer
than a glance. I was also successful at getting him to do
some simple tasks with me. For instance, there was this
cute little sit-on car in the room, and I rolled it over to him
while he was sitting about fifteen feet away from me. I
nonchalantly said, "You used to ride your school bus
when you were at home, why don't you get on that car
and ride it over here for a sip of juice." To my amazement, he hopped right on and drove it over to me, even
paying attention to steer it around a rug. He also showed
me how to beat his drum and play with his construction
man.

When time was up, I took him down to the room
with the beds. Tanaka took a good-bye picture of us; and
then offered to drive me back to the hotel and to bring Jordan along. Just before we left, Dr. Kitahara pulled up to
say good-bye. She assured me that Jordan was a "clever"
boy and that he would make progress.

I got a little teary in parting, but it didn't seem to
bother Jordan. I think he wanted Tanaka to get the bus
moving again.

In February, Jill makes her second trip to Tokyo. Unlike
my visit, when I was the only American parent there, she has
lots of company. Many parents from the school's International
Division are in town to see their children perform at the "Year
End Celebration." It's a great opportunity for Jill to talk with

this group and to begin forming relationships. The foundation
is being laid for the establishment of a core group of parents
who will help launch the Boston Higashi School in September, a prospect which is increasingly probable with every passing month.

In almost every regard, Jill's visit is significantly more
successful than mine. Not only does she have the bonding experience with the other parents, she also comes home more
convinced than I that Jordan is progressing. She is particularly
impressed with the fact that Jordan is showing interest in
other children—holding the hand of a classmate for long
periods of time during a trip to the zoo, for example. He was
also able to carry out his part of the performance put on by his
class, exhibiting the newly acquired skills of imitation and the
ability to move with a group without physical prompts. Jill is
absolutely firm in her belief that Jordan is in the right place
and that further development will be forthcoming.

From February to July, we receive the monthly tapes,
some photographs, and an occasional correspondence from
the school. It is a strange and powerless feeling, not unlike, I
suppose, that which the parents of the "boy in the bubble"
must have felt; the major difference being that they were at
least able to see their child in the flesh. Our longing for Jordan is somewhat assuaged by the fact that the Boston school
will definitely open in September. Dr. Kitahara, being the
tremendously resourceful person that she is, has enlisted the
support of the professional and political communities of Massachusetts to get her dream off the ground. Psychologist Dr.
Jerome Kagan, neurologist Dr. Paul Hardy, educator Ann
Larkin, and governor's wife Kitty Dukakis become directly involved in her efforts to establish Boston Higashi. Being able to
get this kind of support for this nearly impossible and, to

many, crazy venture only raises Dr. Kitahara's stock with her coterie of devoted American parents that much more. ❋

❋

❋

❋

❋ On an unseasonably cool day in July, 1987, Jill and I are sitting in the Baltimore-Washington Airport, awaiting a flight from New York that will return to us our five-year-old son, whom we haven't seen in five months. As on the day he was born, I'm swimming in a sea of emotion. Of course there is the elation of knowing that we will shortly be holding Jordan. And in my mind is also the recent, joyful realization that our daughter does not have autism. Along with these pleasant thoughts is the relief that this will be the last international reunion our family will have to undergo. And additionally, there is comfort in knowing that we will be getting hands-on instruction in Daily Life therapy during the summer: Dr. Kitahara is sending one of her teachers to stay with us for four weeks, to give us an understanding of the methods being used with Jordan and to ease his transition to home life.

There is a great deal to be thankful for, but, at the same time, I'm scared as hell. Over the past few days I've been remembering my trip to Tokyo: the long periods of time with Jordan when I had absolutely no idea of what to do with him; his negative interactions with children on the playground; my sadness that he wasn't making the kind of progress that I had expected of him, even when he was in a program we knew to be of high quality. And then inside I know that I am grappling with the feeling that I slowly have been giving up hope. When he was away at school, we could look at the tapes we were sent and compose optimistic scenarios for the future, but his daily presence in the house shouldn't take long to shoot holes in that picture. The worst aspect of this will be the differing perspectives that Jill and I will hold on this issue, differences which will no doubt lead to friction.

I am abruptly pulled from these depressing cogitations by Jill's enthusiastic squeal: she's spotted Jordan down on the tarmac, emerging from the little plane that has carried him and his teacher on the last leg of their sojourn from Tokyo. I pop out of my seat to get a view before they enter the tunnel to come into the airport. He and Mrs. Hakarino look extremely bedraggled. No wonder: their journey started two days before, when they arrived at Narita airport only to learn that their flight had been cancelled. They then spent that evening in a hotel at the airport before catching the fifteen-hour flight to New York. From there it was a mile sprint through LaGuardia to barely catch the flight to Baltimore.

No matter: we surround Jordan in a deep family hug that lasts as long as he will bear it, then turn tearfully to welcome Mrs. Hakarino and to thank her for undergoing all that she's been through. "Chiaki" provides us with some of the gory details of the trip as we leave the airport and head for Ellicott City. Jordan has hardly slept the past few days, and, from the looks of her, she hasn't slept at all. Although Chiaki's English is fairly limited, we also get some information about Jordan's life over the past few months as we drive home. She tells us what a good boy Jordan has been, how he sleeps and eats well, how he is learning such things as tracing and using scissors, that he is pleasant and is liked by the nondisabled Japanese children. We listen intently, Jill fairly burying Jordan with affection.

This is Mrs. Hakarino's first trip to the United States, and as we travel along you can tell that she is finding the scale of things here a little hard to fathom. When we arrive in Ellicott City, it becomes apparent that what to us is a modest rancher with a nice yard, can be seen, from another perspective, as a palace in the midst of a forest. Standing on the deck overlooking our back yard, Mrs. Hakarino, ever so slowly, surveys the perimeter of our property. "So much land!" she finally utters. The wonder in her eyes and voice remind me of a time—long ago—when her pupil and I took in that same view, and he said, "So many trees." ❄

❄

❄

❄

❄ Many surprises are in store for this young Japanese woman over the next four weeks, but more are in store for us. The first comes that very night, after we ready Jordan for bed. Following his bath, we begin to lead him away to his room, only to discover that Mrs. Hakarino's plan calls for Jordan to sleep with her in the family room. Even when we point out that the family room has but one bed, she can't be dissuaded from her program. This is dedication of the highest order. It's especially amazing that she's willing to start this regimen on the first night, after having spent the better part of the last forty-eight hours awake.

On the following morning, we receive our second surprise—Jordan's summer school. After breakfast it had been my intention to take Jordan to a nearby playground that had been an old haunt. Nothing doing! Rather, Jordan's instructional day is to begin promptly after the meal, at which time he will pack a backpack with skates, a container of water, and a wet wash cloth in preparation for the morning outing. We discover as the summer goes on that these daily excursions generally consist of a two-mile hike with short breaks for water and longer breaks for roller skating. When skating proves problematic because of the rough surface of the roads, riding a tricycle or a two-wheel bike with training wheels is substituted. The routine never flags, even on those many days when the thermometer reads in excess of 90 degrees.

Observing the preparation for this first in the series of outings would lead to another surprise—the difference between Jordan's behavior with Chiaki and with us. As he would do on almost every other morning of the summer, Jordan barely bats an eye as he embarks on his morning venture. In fact, his entire day—that is, the part that he spends with Chiaki—is a model of compliance. From nine to three, he eats, exercises, goes to the bathroom, watches TV, and does a minimum of forty-five minutes of "homework" without incident. And some of this homework requires a good deal of concentration, such as cutting out shapes, coloring in pictures, or making art projects using glue and small pieces of paper. But turn the reins over to his parents, and then we have a horse of a different color. Willfulness and temper tantrums begin to reemerge, though, admittedly, not quite as bad as they had been the summer before.

The disparity between Jordan's behavior with us and his teacher is disconcerting, but, at the same time, it is encouraging. We think it would be nice if we could exert the same kind of influence that Chiaki does, but seeing her do so at least lets us know that it can be done. And in watching and talking to her we become confident that, at some point, we, too, will be able to work effectively with Jordan. As the summer days pass, we ask for more time to observe her in order that we'll be prepared for the two weeks in August when we will be his only teachers.

And during the final days that Chiaki is with us, as I examine his behavior more closely, I come to realize the summer's final pleasant surprise—Jordan's enhanced abilities and organization. Little, but significant, things are different about him. He can now carry his eating utensils to a designated place; he's willing to put away toys; he will return to pick up things that he's dropped; he doesn't perseverate as much in doing tasks such as puzzles; and he is, in general, more able, i.e., using scissors, fastening his seat belt, writing with a pencil.

But not all of the news of the summer is good. On a sweltering day in August I'm playing with him in the backyard when I notice a ball lying amidst several toys in the sandbox. Thinking I might be able to show him how to play catch, I ask him to bring it to me, but he reaches down and picks up a toy car instead. To see if this is a random mistake or a pattern, I then ask him to bring me his truck. Again he picks up the wrong object. Later, at dinner, I check his understanding of the names of other familiar objects, such as plates and different kinds of foods, and the result is the same. When we mention our concerns to Ms. Hakarino, she dismisses them, saying that Jordan not only understands many English nouns but some Japanese as well. For me, though, the answer seems clear. The final nail is in place; he is a boy without nouns.

For several days I try to fathom this situation, wondering, though I could see it coming for a long time, how he could have lost virtually all of his language when everyone told us that he'd improve. Throughout this period of nearly three years, psychologists, neurologists, self-styled autism gurus, teachers (American and Japanese), relatives and friends, even our own intuitions had joined in a continuing chorus of "We Shall Overcome." Now the harmony is gone, the tune is flat, and the voices are silent.

"In the beginning was the word, and the word was with God, and the word was God," so goes the quote from the Book of John. In this familiar passage from our culture's most widely read book, we have a succinct but eloquent summary of what is most fundamental about being human. Similar expressions of this idea are found in other religious traditions, too. It is universally accepted that God is in the word. Parents receive a first-hand experience of the meaning of this notion when their children make their initial utterances. When Jordan spoke his first words, it was a spiritual moment that rivalled any that I had known up to that point. It heralded the onset of communication; it signalled the potential for forming relationships; it represented the beginning of a process that would lead to his full admission to the human family. Now, though, every word is gone, and like some long suffering throwback to the Old Testament, I have seen my first-born son taken from me to Babylon, where everyone talks to him in tongues. And as if to add mockery to his cruelty, this inscrutable God dresses up his newly mute creation in a cherubic and intelligent looking face that would only later, as the only doctor who seemed to recognize Jordan's future suggested, "begin to look more retarded."

These gnawing thoughts boil up inside me as round and round the black, synthetic track I circle in the throbbing heat of an August night. I am in the midst of my ritualistic effort to maintain a meaningless health. Two, three, four miles I run, my feet almost parting the earth with the intense gravity of my steps. The final two hundred yards I sprint in anger, forcing myself to the limit. As I stop and cool down, I look to the sky in the way I had done some two and a half years before after the first session with the neurologist, when a brilliant sunset, seeming like the face of God Himself, played midwife to the accouchement of my prayer for understanding. But there is nothing to pray for now. A tiny light, perhaps from the Perseid meteor shower, flickers in a corner of the sky and dies. Here is the perfect metaphor for Jordan. In the backdrop of an empty sky, he moved so brilliantly and then passed from the scene in an instant. Twinkle, twinkle little star, now I wonder where you are.

V

$\mathscr{T}$he final two weeks of the summer pass. It is September, the start of another school year. Now Jordan is a student at Boston Higashi School, and things are very different from the way they were when he was in Tokyo. We have, of course, the comfort of realizing that Jordan is only an eight-hour drive away. We also know that there will be some parents there who have either moved to the Boston area over the summer or who were residents of that part of the country before. They will provide some supplement to the school's reports of Jordan's development. Additionally, four American teachers have been hired to work at the school, and one of them will be working on a daily basis with Jordan as his primary teacher. Given our concerns about Jordan's language regression, knowing that he will be spoken to in his native tongue every day is particularly important to us.

In general, it's markedly easier for us to stay focused on other elements of our lives during the 1987-1988 school year. Aiding greatly in this process is the fact that two of our major concerns of the year before seem to be coming to favorable resolutions. First, we are absolutely certain that Leslie does not have autism. By the end of 1987 even the pediatrician is making this claim. And we also now have a plan for taking care of our funding problem, a plan which actually began to take shape during the summer.

After learning that the tuition for a residential student at Boston Higashi would exceed $30,000 for the first year, and would likely be higher after that, we realize that we've nothing to lose by vigorously pursuing public funding. After all, the federal special education law states clearly that Jordan has a right to a "free and appropriate" education, and he is clearly getting this at Higashi at a cost comparable to or less than what would be found at any school in which he would be placed by our county. Ostensibly, then, there would be no reason for our jurisdiction not to fund Higashi.

Thinking along these lines, Jill develops a strategy. First, we will go through all of the necessary evaluations, scheduling them during the period that Chiaki will be home with us. It's clear to us, after seeing how effective she is at getting him to stay on task, that having her present at these evaluations will enable us to demonstrate in a dramatic way the appropriateness of the Higashi program. The county's "testing crew" will be able to match their ability to get Jordan to cooperate against that of Chiaki, and the starkness of the contrast should make it evident that something in the Higashi program is working. At the same time, we will solicit recommendations from our own doctors that Jordan be in a level 6 (residential) placement. Actually, there is little question that this type of placement is appropriate, given Jordan's behavior at home: his frequent tantrums, flat-out uncooperativeness, disruptive sleeping problems, and penchant for constantly roaming around the house, picking up and often destroying everything that isn't nailed down. All of the reports that we gather from our medical team wind up including that recommendation, as well as suggestions that Jordan's continued placement at Higashi is in his best interest.

With this documentation in hand, our meeting with the special education team goes well. It is agreed that Jordan's recommended placement be Higashi. All that awaits the funding of Jordan's education is having Boston Higashi approved by the state of Maryland. But what seems like a simple matter for final resolution, will ultimately be sixteen months and a legal battle in the making. As someone once said, "If God wanted laws to be followed, he wouldn't have created lawyers." More on this later. With our impending legal battles not yet apparent, however, the school year's start seems to show things coming together for us. We have a healthy daughter growing more interactive by the day; we have a quality educational placement for Jordan, which, very soon, should stop costing us our retirement; and we have jump-started our careers. Jill has been promoted to deputy chief of her division, and I have taken a central office position with the potential for increasing my ability to affect school policy district wide. But when you have a child with autism, you become like the little Dutch boy, plugging up the sea wall with your thumb. Every time you plug a hole, the wall seems to sprout another leak, eventually leaving you with a depleted supply of appendages.

In October, Jill makes her first visit of the school year to Boston, and from that point on whatever tenuous hold on peace we have begins to erode. Things get off to a bad start when she arrives to find Jordan sick again. This is our third visit in a little over a year, and each time we've had to spend at least part of the visit playing nurse. Never anything serious, just colds, but the consistency is a little disconcerting. We wonder whether he gets proper nourishment, or if he gets enough to drink, or if the dorm is kept too warm, or if he simply stays in a state of perpetual infection due to constant proximity with other kids. Jill also reports that he seems less active—though this might be a by-product of the cold—and that no cognitive or language improvements are apparent.

Other problems come to the fore during Jill's visit as well. For example, she learns that the recently hired American teachers are already dissatisfied with the working environment at Higashi, and there's talk of quitting. Additionally, very little has been done by the school's administration to get Boston Higashi on Maryland's approved list of schools, so there seems little likelihood that we'll be getting funding in the near future.

Shortly after her return, these circumstances give Jill an idea that would prove as problematic to our relationship as it was implacable. Through the middle of this idea would run a fault line ever threatening to crack and draw us all in. In brief, Jill comes to the conclusion that Jordan is becoming a child apart from his family; that his development is being retarded as a result of this; and that this alienation is creating family tensions greater than any which would be created if Jordan was living at home with one or both of us.

The solution that springs from this logic is for one or both of us to move to Massachusetts. The final draft of this plan calls for me to move to Massachusetts by myself, get established in a school district, and have Jordan move in with me. Jill would then follow and find work as a lawyer.

I agree with Jill's first point. It is obviously going to be exceedingly difficult for Jordan to maintain a relationship with people he doesn't see but once a month. But Point A does not necessarily lead to Point B or Point C for me. After having had the summer to see how ineffective both of us are with him, I disagree that his progress is retarded in our absence. And, as far as family solidarity goes, the current arrangement seems like the only sensible solution. How could we pack up and move without jobs? What guarantee would there be that we'd find a town that would fund the school? What would be the effect on Leslie of having Jordan live at home? No, this doesn't sound like a prescription for mental health so much as it sounds like a program for family meltdown. ❄

❄

❄

❄

❄ Einstein was reportedly fond of saying, "God may be subtle, but he is not malicious." Members of my family, however, might justifiably reverse the adjectives in that aphorism. Take Thanksgiving, 1987, as a case in point.

A cool gray day opens up before me as I step out of the house and kiss Jill and the baby good-bye. I'm headed for New Jersey, stopping over at my brother's on the way to spend a couple of days with Jordan. Curt and a friend have spent the night before with my mother, so everyone will rendezvous there before driving on to Asbury Park to have Thanksgiving dinner at his place later that evening. As I had expected, traffic is considerably lighter now than it would have been the night before, and within two hours I'm turning off the interstate for the final ten miles of the trip. I'm following along Route 130, a road that I've driven since my high school cruising days. Never a lovely stretch of highway, today its gloom and decay are inescapable. Boarded-up buildings, trash, grime, and the general effects of neglect are everywhere. This prototypical picture of America's post-industrial outback looks as if it yearns to return to its former life as a meadow, the state it had been in in the days of my father's boyhood.

It's a relief to be finally off that godforsaken road when I turn onto my mother's street. But even here the decline is obvious. And the deterioration is not limited to the buildings. Recently, there have occurred two violent deaths on the very block on which I'm driving. As I stop the car, I think how much I hate having Mom live alone in this area. And even though she has put the house up for sale, I worry that she won't find a qualified buyer to move into such a tainted neighborhood.

I shut the motor off and try to shut down my unpleasant thoughts while I make my way to the door. I realize something is wrong when my custom of making a loud and obnoxious entry into the short foyer doesn't elicit the usual response. And when I push open the door leading into the living room, it becomes apparent that something is dramatically amiss. I don't have to wait long for an explanation as my mother tells me that my first cousin's husband (a member of the Camden, New Jersey, police force) has been shot and critically wounded earlier that morning. Throughout the rest of the day it is touch and go, but eventually it becomes evident that he will survive. Something to be thankful for.

Later that evening my brother, his friend, my mother, and I sit in my brother's living room listening silently to George Winston's "December" album. Against the dimly lit backdrop, the sad piano refrain underscores the chasm between the start of the holiday season and the continuing demise of our spirits. But the events of the past two years, looming large in our minds that evening, would prove to be only the tip of the iceberg. Unbeknownst to me on that night, my brother, who appears the picture of health, lies in the initial stage of HIV infection. Unbeknownst to all of us, my nearly widowed cousin would soon lose a baby, and almost lose her mother to cancer. And, incredibly, within two years her only sister—seven months pregnant at the time—would lose her husband to a freak household accident. ❄

❄

❄

❄

❋ "Honey, we're back!" I plop the mail and groceries on the kitchen table and pull off Leslie's home-made "Big Bird" jacket. It's been an unusually warm March day, and I've been buoyed by the thought of spring's approach. Jill seems happy too as she picks up Leslie on her way into the kitchen. "Some prospective buyers were here this morning. I think they were very interested," she announces as if to accentuate her resolve to carry out the plan to sell the house. Lately this plan has definitely metamorphosed into the option I've considered most extreme, that calling for Jordan and me to live together in Boston while she and Leslie stay in Maryland.

I direct my attention to the mail to avoid rehashing old arguments. Among the usual pile of catalogs and bills is the *Autism Research Review International*, a quarterly periodical which highlights studies related to autism and is put out by autism expert Bernard Rimland, whose pioneering work helped establish the biological bases of autism. On page four is a report on a study done by Japanese and American researchers who tracked the development of children with late and early onset autism. The findings of this study represent the first piece of information I've seen that is consistent with Jordan's development. The researchers found that children with delayed onset autism were actually far more at risk of abnormal social development and of remaining or becoming mentally retarded than those whose symptoms appeared shortly after birth. In fact, 90 percent of those with late onset autism were either hospitalized or attending schools for the mentally handicapped, while over 60 percent of the children with early onset autism were going to ordinary schools.

I read the article twice before handing it over to Jill with the introduction, "Here is our answer." Jill reads through the article with interest, but disagrees that this necessarily means anything terribly significant. "You always do this, Craig: you read one study, and suddenly you know everything." Subsequent issues of the journal, however, would provide additional evidence that autistic children who, like Jordan, lost speech and cognitive skills, were at far greater risk than those children whose acquisition of skills was merely delayed.

Having seen this article, I am at once relieved and dismayed. On the one hand, I now believe that nothing we have done has caused Jordan to decline, and, correspondingly, that there was probably little that could have been done to prevent what happened to him. But the small relief I can take from this knowledge is swamped by the overwhelming feeling of helplessness that the information brings.

Throughout that afternoon, I feel immobilized by this revelation. Jill, ever alert to swings in my mood, gets after me about my attitude, but I am impervious to the criticism and the call to action. What's more, Jill's plan to have me move to Boston and care for Jordan by myself seems especially absurd in the light of this new information. Before the night is out, we are arguing vociferously in front of my in-laws, sucking them into the maelstrom of tension that would grip us like forceps from that time right up to our eventual move a year later.

Not long after our "Fort Sumter," Jill relinquishes her frontal assault strategy to conduct a campaign of attrition. First, she takes the house off the market, reasoning that even if I am living in Boston, she might be better off staying in the house rather than living with her parents. Next, she agrees to consider the advice of others before finalizing the decision to move. I'm particularly interested in seeking the opinions of our medical people and of the other families we know with autistic children, especially Fran and Monroe Lerner, the couple whose high functioning, adult son we had met at the autism society picnic three years before. ❄

❄

❄

❄

❄ In May, we bring Jordan home for medical evaluations, and take this rare opportunity of having him in Maryland to visit the Lerners. Not having seen Jordan in quite a while, they are very impressed with his improved sociability and with the fact that he seems calmer and happier. They notice that he comes to us when we call and that he will try to vocalize in response to our questions. Seeing these changes in him, they express confidence that our decision to place Jordan at Higashi was correct. But they also share with us a very definite opinion that splitting up the family so that Jordan can live with me is a dubious proposition at best.

Jill greatly respects the Lerners, and this opinion lays to rest the plan to have me move to Boston by myself. This thought alone gives me the strength to face the summer, which is good, because things will be considerably different this year: we will not have a Japanese teacher to come home with Jordan. We will be on our own to fill the days, totally responsible for keeping him on track. ❄

❄

❄

❄

❄ Columbia, Maryland's, Lake Elkhorn is a hazy, tranquil pool on this inferno of an August afternoon. Across the way, some barely distinguishable swans are gliding motionlessly along the shore. Jordan and I are on a daring "out of air conditioning" mission to kill time on this day when almost nothing else is moving. And, at the pace we are traveling, a whole afternoon should have been slain by the time we've gone completely around the lake. Later on, we'll cool off and let more of the day evaporate at the park playground: Jordan sitting calmly in the swing, and I counting the pushes. Maybe we'll reach a thousand before supper.

My partner and I are getting used to this sort of thing; filling up the days of the seven-week vacation. It is as if the mere act of living has become a task, and for four weeks now, we have approached this task with uniform resignation. This time at home has been very different from past vacations. More and more, Jordan is expressionless, rarely showing excitement, except on some occasions at the YMCA pool. Spending time with him is like being handed an ancient text, written in a language no longer spoken. To break the code might yield untold wonders, but not knowing where to start simply unleashes a torrent of frustration. His language shows no progress. He can understand some simple directions, but he never says any words. Even the range of sounds he makes has been reduced. For example, he never makes the "k" or "g" sounds, and seems incapable of imitating them. And, if he wants something, he makes his needs known by pointing. Improvements in other areas are negligible. And he is exceedingly difficult to engage, despite his surprising willingness to go through the motions for many activities. At times he is so fully immersed in some self-stimulatory activity such as breaking sticks that he is difficult to contact, at other times he is so aware of his surroundings that he bolts away from you, even when you approach him quietly from behind.

Though many, like Jill, believe he is still benefitting from the education he is receiving at Higashi, I am increasingly skeptical. To me, his behavior is robotic, devoid of personality or animation. I remind myself that he could be aggressive, or self-injurious, or more prone to temper tantrums; that at least he is more manageable. But without much hope that Jordan can learn to communicate, I begin to wonder about the point of his life.

Fortunately, the summer passes before my poisonous attitude leads to permanent neurasthenia. For there is heavy psychological work ahead in this, our final, year in Maryland. Despite my concern that Jordan is not making the kind of progress I'd hoped for, I still feel that Higashi is a better program than any that would be offered by our jurisdiction. We have visited one residential school for children with autism located in our county, for example, and the teachers did not seem to be making much of an effort with their students. One teacher explained to Jill that if the students chose not to pay attention, she did not take aggressive action to change the situation. Not exactly a prescription for success. I feel, too, that the principal of Higashi is correct in her belief that Jordan would be better off as a day student. It is also becoming evident that Maryland is unlikely to ever put Higashi on its list of approved placements for autistic children. Because the school failed to meet some regulatory requirements—apparently etched in stone—a visiting contingent of Maryland special education officials rejected Higashi's application in the spring. Without that approval, it will be exceedingly difficult for us to get state funding; and without the funding, we will be faced with financial ruin. A move to Massachusetts seems inevitable.

These realizations notwithstanding, however, our impending move to Massachusetts will not be entirely without problems. The issue of jobs remains foremost. Jill will likely be able to transfer her legal skills to some position of comparable pay and responsibility. She will, however, be required to go through a lot of preliminary steps to make her eligible for any such employment. My situation should prove more problematic. Having been in contact with the Massachusetts Department of Education for some time now, I am aware that my teaching certificate will transfer. But I won't, as I would have been in Maryland, be eligible for an administrative job, since no reciprocal agreement exists between the two states in this area of certification. Essentially, this means that I'll be limited to classroom teacher positions when I apply. Even getting a classroom teaching position won't be a given, however, since many jurisdictions will rule me out because they'd have to pay me considerably more than they would an applicant right out of college. And should I get such a job, I'll be working sixty-hour weeks and getting paid less. The thought of undertaking this kind of responsibility, along with taking care of Jordan in the evening, seems daunting to say the least.

The start of the 1988-89 school year presents us with more immediate problems, though. We want to take care of the bills we have been facing every month. For the past year, we have been sending nearly $4,000 a month to Higashi to cover the cost of Jordan's education. Because of the verbal agreement we had had with our county, and the overwhelming approval of Jordan's placement among those consulting in his case, we were willing to pay that bill in the belief that we would some day recoup what we'd paid. By the fall of 1988, however, it seems unlikely that we will ever see a penny of the money, and the costs for the current school year will be in excess of $4,000 a month.

Since Jordan's education is supposed to be free and appropriate, there doesn't seem to be any reason why we shouldn't be approved for funding, especially since no alternative placement has ever been seriously presented to us. This fact that we didn't receive counsel about other options could prove to be the focal point of a case which Jill believes we would win if we had to take Maryland to court. But the first step in protecting our rights in this process—as any good lawyer knows—is to get a good lawyer.

Because Jill is such a lawyer, it proves relatively easy for us to obtain such a lawyer. Though never actually going to court, our "case" drags on for a couple of months, and a good number of hoops and meetings must be endured. But eventually we get our hearing, where our lawyer makes the state officials look like fools. The upshot of months of wrangling is a settlement, the facts and details of which must remain secret. Looks like another case of lawyers cleaning up the details. Even after we essentially have our moment of redress, however, it's months before we see the fruit.

At any rate, however, the central question around which our family's future has revolved for the past year—whether and when to move to Massachusetts—seems resolved as we mark the fourth anniversary of autism in December of 1988. Two events make the move virtually inevitable. First, there is the finalization of our settlement with Maryland. In the form that it takes, this agreement makes it almost impossible that Maryland will fund Higashi in the future. Second, there is the continuing pressure from Dr. Kitahara for Jordan to become a day student. She makes a point of reminding us of her feeling about this issue when we pick him up at Christmas.

Sitting in the school's lobby with her assistant, Ms. Takako Saegusa, and her interpreter, Ms. Takako Oe, Dr. Kitahara smiles softly as we wait for Jordan's teacher to bring him up from his classroom. Ms. Oe translates easily as Dr. Kitahara summarizes Jordan's progress over the first semester in her quiet, steady voice. "We think Jordan is making good progress. His behavior is becoming less and less severe, and he enjoys being with his friends at school. But we think he would make even better progress, especially in learning to talk, if he lived at home. He is definitely ready to leave the dormitory."

When I bring up my concerns about Jordan's regression, she just smiles and shakes her head as if to say "No way."

Just when the issue seems settled, Boston Higashi faces a threat to its very existence in the form of three deaths. Two are students, both deaths occurring in the dormitory during the 1988-89 school year. And although both are determined to be the result of natural causes, with the school bearing no responsibility for this terrible, freak coincidence, questions are raised about the quality of care and teaching methods being practiced at Higashi. These questions continue to dog the school and create in its leadership concerns about the survivability of the operation which would not be dispelled until a couple of years later. The third death, coming on January 14th, 1989, stuns the parents, friends, and staff of Higashi. On that day, Boston Higashi loses its founder, Dr. Kiyo Kitahara.

The death of a fledgling organization's leader during a critical period of development would be a difficult blow for any operation to survive. The fact that Dr. Kitahara dies in this year of crisis, however, makes the threat to the school's ability to carry on even more pronounced. Upon hearing of her death, I wonder whether there will be sufficient will among the Japanese staff to stay in a country that has proven to be such a quagmire for them. Throughout the period of crisis, however, the American parents rally behind the school, and, by the annual Year End Celebration in June, it's clear that Boston Higashi will open as scheduled next fall.

During this same period, other events in Maryland are also conspiring to ensure that we will, at least temporarily, move to Massachusetts. Because of the uncertainties in what we were doing, it had been my feeling that we should take leaves of absence from our jobs rather than tendering resigna-

tions. The thinking was that we didn't want to pile the
prospect of long-term financial headaches on top of the stresses related to relocating and having Jordan rejoin the family
on a full-time basis. Since I had recently had a leave of absence, though, I felt certain that I would have trouble in ob-
taining another. But this proves no hurdle at all as my
application is easily approved.

Jill's case is even better. She arranges to keep her job in
Maryland, agreeing to work ten or so days every month there,
while completing the rest of her work at home in Massachusetts during the remainder of the month. This arrangement will allow us to keep about 60 percent of our income,
even if I can't find any work at all. Thus, the final brick is in
place. All that remains is to decide whether to sell or rent our
current home. It's a pretty good market, so we sell, and before
we have left for the Bay State, we agree on an acceptable
offer. ❄

❄

❄

❄

❄ At the same time we are working out the logistical and
financial details that will allow us to move to Massachusetts, I
am undergoing something of a spiritual crisis. In retrospect, I
think this is because I was exceedingly battle weary by this
point. In fact, it is not too difficult to draw some parallels between what Jill and I had undergone in struggling with autism
and what the soldiers in the Civil War had to endure. Obviously, we did not have to endure the incredible hardship
and deprivation that Civil War combatants did, nor did we
have to witness the unconscionable horror of mass death. But

the sense of frustration at having participated in an unabated fight over a long period of time in which there had been no real winners, the beholding of life with promise being snuffed out, the suffering of disruption and division in our family; these experiences we held in common with our nineteenth-century forbearers.

By the time that Jordan had left to return to school in the summer of 1988, we had known autism for almost four years. Like Robert E. Lee and his Army of Northern Virginia compatriots, we had taken pains to research our enemy, we had strategized, we had built up the morale of our forces, and we had waged an assiduous campaign with every willingness to suffer casualties. But in the end, we were simply outgunned. The total, and seemingly irrevocable, loss of Jordan's ability to communicate, which we could be certain of by this time, presented the psychological equivalent of Pickett's Charge: a series of skirmishes in a pointless war of attrition seemed all that was left. When the fighting was over, however, the Confederates could at least return home. For us, there would be nothing to which we could surrender.

In this last year in Maryland, I am acutely aware that I must begin a process of self-healing. Both our existing and pending responsibilities call for a different perspective than the one I am manifesting. I see my daughter, now two and a half years old, talking and becoming more attuned to her surroundings. I see Jill maintaining a fighting spirit. I think of the considerable efforts of the staff at Higashi. I recall all of the sacrifices that my family, friends, and others have made on behalf of Jordan, and I realize that I need to come to terms with my despair. Awareness of a need and arrival at a solution to address it are, regrettably, points at vast distances apart.

I am in a quandary about where to begin. I can take no relief in religion: I don't believe in a personal God. I can't pour myself into my career: I am moving further away from a focus in this area and am not even sure what I'll be doing in a year. And I feel as if I'm too private a person to benefit from psychological counseling. But though I don't believe I'll be able to take advantage of these traditional avenues of healing, I have a basic faith in the universe and myself. What I need, then, is a vehicle for refocusing this positive sense about life that, if not always with me, has been at least accessible to my psyche in times of crisis.

Two things, it seems, are necessary in this regard: a mindset which will redirect my emotional energies away from thoughts of Jordan, and a means for sustaining that mindset. In my situation, a Christian would focus on his ultimate salvation as a means for preserving his mental health against the vicissitudes of fate. And the vehicle for maintaining that perspective could be prayer, reading the Bible, attending church or others. A Buddhist would, obviously, have a different perspective and use different techniques. Unconsciously, I am drawn to an alternative path, one whose nature only emerges after I'm fully involved with it. In essence, my choice is to reduce my own ego, by drawing the universe around me into sharper focus while allowing the events in my own life to become a backdrop. The regimen I choose for trying to maintain this outlook is reading.

In one way or another, bibliotherapy has played a significant role in my life since high school, when my first exposure to literature brought me in touch with whole new ways of thinking. And throughout my adult life prior to autism, I had continued this literary habit, though most of my reading revolved around utilitarian purposes such as professional development. In this period, however, when I have time on my hands and trouble in my heart, I am instinctively drawn to science. I reason that if I can find reading material which is not too technical, but which can take me to the threshold of our current understanding of how the universe began, how life evolved, and how consciousness developed, I might find a sense of peace in being involved with—if only as an observer—humanity's quest for roots. Additionally, I am aware that scientific understanding has already extended to the most distant past and the farthest reaches of space; that it has partially unveiled the nature of the very large and the very small; and that it has begun to sketch the outlines of the story of life and thought itself. Ironically, not long after embarking on this mental journey, I encountered an idea expressed by historian Thomas Berry, which summed up my intuition about this matter. In his book, *The Dream of Earth*, Berry made the assertion that the scientific account of the universe is the moral and spiritual event of the century.

I must say, in retrospect, that the hours I spent reading the writings of scientists and science writers like Louise Young, Paul Davies, Ilya Prigogene, Steven Hawking, Lynn Margulis, Robert Shapiro, and others, not only brought a different focus to my mental energies, it also awakened me to the astonishing capacities of the universe. In the book, *The Unfinished Universe*, Louise Young gives the most succinct and compelling expression to the modern ideas emerging from scientific investigation. Here she characterizes the universe as an evolving hierarchy of self-organizing forms—of beings like multicellular organisms that evolve on their own into more complex forms. It is a process whose end cannot be known, but one which does not necessarily have to result in total entropy. The world of theoretical biology, physics, and math is also uncovering strange phenomenon and concepts such as holograms (laser-created images that take advantage of the properties of wave interference to create complete images from wave fragments), chaos theory (the mathematically derived theory that all dynamic processes are subject to unpredictable fluctuations that make them difficult to understand or predict), and Lynn Margulis's theory that all complex organisms evolved through a process of cooperation among microorganisms.

What this phase of my bibliotherapy accomplishes for me is a sense of wonder about the processes of the universe. I come away, too, with the strengthened belief that nature operates on the principle of cooperation, played out on a field of interconnectedness, leading to increasing complexity and beauty. Having this sense can help in turning one's head from the self to the other, in much the same way that traditional religion can. I become aware over time, however, that it will take more than this knowledge alone to sustain that selfless perspective. I will need to take advantage of the world's stockpile of spiritual insight in order to reach the next level.

In this second phase of reading, my interest focuses on those religious traditions with which I am least familiar. The wisdom of Judeo-Christianity—though no doubt of considerable comfort to many—has never provided me with the foundation upon which I can construct cathedrals of inner peace. I want to learn about the religious traditions of non-western peoples, to explore the basic ideas of ancient belief systems whose views on the nature and creation of the universe seem so closely related to the modern scientific perspective. My guides in this area are many, but, to my way of thinking, no writer is better able to explain the philosophies of Hinduism, Buddhism, and Zen than Nancy Wilson-Ross.

In her book, *The Three Ways of Asian Wisdom*, Wilson-Ross brings to her readers the treasure trove of religious thought coming from the east. Her valuable insights about each tradition, served up in an inspirational prose, help me to develop a perspective on the recent events of my life, and to imbue my experience with meaning.

Hinduism, the original fountain of spiritual wisdom out of Asia, is the launching pad for my inner space travel. Hinduism provides, first, an alternative way of looking at my specific problem—living with the paradox of having known Jordan as both a happy, healthy, and connected toddler, and as a sad, isolated, and declining child. The answer it offers is the simple recognition that paradoxical elements lie at the heart of the mystery of life itself, and that the understanding and acceptance of this truth is the only path to peace.

Hinduism can be of assistance in facing up to what existentialists might call life's "thrownness," or those conditions over which one has little control. But, at least for me, it is an outlook that is difficult to maintain in the face of the perceived suffering of loved ones. I might look at my own circumstance and say, "I see the beauty and joy of the world, and I am fortunate enough to have an active mind that can carry me away from myself; that can conceive of a strategy that allows me to accept the world as it is." But what about Jordan? He seems terribly unhappy at times, and he has no way of controlling his reaction to his surroundings; no way of superimposing on life a belief system that can explain away his pain. Enter Buddhism to add another support to a searching philosophy.

According to Buddhism, there is no such thing as "I"—no such thing as a separate self. If I am saddened by the notion that Jordan is suffering, it is only because I don't fully understand that his existence as a single, solid thing is a Chimera. Reduced to its essentials, "consciousness," from the Buddhist perspective, is merely a collection of attributes, a collection which they call "skandhas."

If Buddhism is accepted, though, why should anyone be-come involved in the world? What possible advantage can be obtained by introducing an act of will into a seamless web of energy flow that is continuously evaporating? The form of Buddhism called Zen has a response to this conundrum. Ac-cording to Zen, involvement in the world is not meaningless. Rather, only those actions which are taken on behalf of the ego are to be avoided. For me, the message is clear: attend to the present, enjoy the experience of consciousness, continue to work with Jordan, but don't read too much into the results. Instead, let the inner workings of the universe proceed, absent my ego.

All of this information that I have absorbed over this period of intense outreach to the world of the mind must, however, be filtered through my mental processes. Life con-tinues to go on, and I cannot step outside of myself into some world of ideas and still participate in that life as I must. Despite the wonders of nature and the universe, I have dif-ficulty in closing my eyes to the problems that Jordan and, for that matter, most of humanity faces. Consciousness would seem to be a gift of little value if its primary effect is to render one capable of experiencing pain. Further, though the wisdom of the ages exhorts us to concentrate on the here and now, it is hard not to worry about how we as a family will get along in the future when we seem to be putting so many stressors into our lives. And even if I can accept Buddhism's ultimate truth that there is no such thing as the self, I cannot bring this pearl of wisdom down deep into my heart to convince it that this bundle of perceptions doesn't form an entity. They may only be skandhas, but they're my skandhas.

In the summer of 1989, my bundle of perceptions is wondering whether continuing on in its present form is worth doing. Hours spent getting nowhere trying to teach Jordan,

countless times seeing his face screwed up in unhappy pos-
tures, daily battles over entering stores or leaving playgrounds,
have brought me to the edge on this quiet August night. Our
doctor friend, Jeff, is visiting with us. He listens patiently as I
predict untold disasters resulting from our impending move to
Massachusetts. Jill sits by, biting her lip, looking as if she
would rather be biting mine. Jeff knows of our differences on
this issue and, because he is an old friend, uses his experience
from past negotiations to help us diffuse the bomb. The anger
in our voices subsides under Jeff's calming effect, but the mood
of the night is captured in our final exchange. Half seriously, I
question Jeff as to whether he knows of any painless ways of
committing suicide. He parries the thought away with his
usual good humor, but he and Jill are aware that I've devoted
some thought to this issue. Neither of them acts as if the idea
is totally outrageous when I point out that Jill and Leslie
would be free to carry on with their lives in a semi-normal
way if Jordan and I were "liberated." They do assure me,
though, that they think it's too soon to give up hope. ✳

                                        ✳

                            ✳

                 ✳

    ✳ Three weeks later, we have moved to Acton, Mas-
sachusetts, a town about twenty-five miles west of Boston. On
Labor Day weekend I am walking around Walden Pond with
Jordan. One hundred and forty years before, Thoreau walked
these same woods and had, among other thoughts, the idea
that most men lead lives of quiet desperation. The faces that I
see on the beach and along the narrow path that circles this
pond don't look desperate, though. I, on the other hand, seem

to fit fairly well what the philosopher of Concord had in mind. I'm, in fact, almost hyperventilating on this hike as thoughts of my situation begin to coalesce. I'm almost forty; I'm about to put another hole in my resume; I've moved to one of the most expensive areas in the country (a move made doubly problematic by the fact that the area's economy is about to go on a tremendous skid, which will make it more difficult for me to find work when I do start to look); I'm going to be without my wife and daughter for ten to twelve days a month for an indefinite period of time; and I will be alone with Jordan for many more hours than I'm used to.

The last of these circumstances is probably as much of a concern to me as any of the rest. Lately, Jordan has been very difficult to deal with, especially in the area of self-control. For example, if we limit the number of times he may open the refrigerator door, or if we try to get him to do a structured activity like stacking blocks, or if we go somewhere he doesn't want to be, he becomes very angry. Sometimes that anger takes the form of hitting, spitting, or biting. At other times, it is directed inward and he bangs his wrists together so hard you can hear the bones cracking.

It has gotten to the point that I often feel that taking Jordan anywhere risks making me appear a child abuser. Now that he is seven years old, a public temper tantrum for no apparent reason looks a little suspicious. And occasionally during the past summer, I have actually suspected that people were calling the police or social services after witnessing one of our family episodes. On one such occasion at the post office, Jordan starts hitting me very hard with his fists as we stand in line. When I take him out of the line, he cries out loudly and starts to pinch me. When I fail to calm him down by talking softly, I have to practically drag him to the car. Once I'm in the car and pulling away, I notice that the woman who was behind us in line has gotten into her car and is pulling out right behind us. She follows us for several blocks and, at a stoplight, writes something down, looking up at the back of my car as she does so. For several hours after I arrive home, I worry that the police will be arriving any minute. . . . Unfortunately, *Rain Man* has not made everyone aware of the characteristics of people with autism. This situation makes me wonder whether I'm about to become a prisoner in my own home.

In this frame of mind, I often think of the Eskimo word "ayornamut," meaning "it can't be helped." Indeed, during the first couple of weeks in Massachusetts, this word swims in my stream of consciousness. Why this idea should stick in my mind seems to be related to the fact that I am entering a period when I'll have lots of opportunities for reflection, no immediate pressure to do anything, and no definite idea of how I'll work with Jordan or handle my unemployed status. Like some Eskimo, holed up in his igloo in the middle of winter, I feel temporarily safe, but unable to affect much of anything. According to my understanding of modern psychology, these are the conditions in which ulcers thrive. I fully expect our "experiment" in Massachusetts to go poorly, and am thus prepared for the worst. But my apocalyptic visions aren't realized. What actually happens is that things start off well. Even before we have arrived in the state, we are fortunate to find a nice house to rent, for a reasonable price, in a town whose special education officials readily accept Boston Higashi as the appropriate placement for Jordan. Upon moving in, we learn of the many nice features of our neighborhood, including plenty of nearby playgrounds, friendly neighbors, the availability of several children as playmates for Leslie, and a library within walking distance of the house. What's more, we have a remarkable landlord who is prompt in attending to things when they go wrong, and totally non-intrusive otherwise.

Other things start to fall into place as well. Within a month of our move, we have settlement on our house in Maryland, thus alleviating us of our worry about the contract falling through. Additionally, at about the same time, another Higashi family moves into the area from out of state. We have known Ben and Joanne since our boys were classmates in Tokyo in 1986, and their family situation and personalities are very compatible with ours. They even have a daughter who is close enough in age to be a playmate for Leslie. Having them as companions would prove of immeasurable benefit to our mental health from then to this writing.

And, beyond all of this, we begin to notice positive changes in Jordan, the most immediate and dramatic of which is a reduction in tantrums. Right up until the day we moved, Jordan was as likely as not to be unhappy with any situation requiring him to participate in an organized activity. He was also, as mentioned before, very unpredictable in public places, frequently becoming visibly and vocally annoyed without the slightest provocation. But, very suddenly, things change in Massachusetts. For example, he no longer violently shuns activities such as doing puzzles, tracing letters with a pencil, or playing songs on his electronic keyboard (we would point out the keys to push, and he would touch them to produce the song). On some days, he's actually involved in such activities for periods of up to an hour. And his public outbursts drop off considerably, both in quantity and intensity.

Not only is he more cooperative, he's also more interactive. Out in the back yard, at the swing set, he can frequently be seen trying to get the attention of his sister; at dinner he is alerting us through gestures as to what he wants to eat; and at bedtime he is giving us real hugs.

And on an after-school walk in early October, I start to notice a third change: the beginnings of language. It's a glorious day, with the leaves showing a touch of color and the sky a uniform blue. Jordan has just returned from school in one of the town's special education station wagons. The driver, whom we call "Betty Arrival," (in contrast with her morning namesake, "Betty Departure,") has a smile on her face and a positive report as she lets Jordan out of the car. He has been a pleasant boy on the ride home, laughing frequently and apparently showing signs of knowing where he was as the car turned onto our street. When the car comes to a stop, Jordan has no time for greetings or good-byes; he immediately heads for the backyard to play on the swing set. I spend a minute or two talking to Betty, and then decide I'd better check on what Jordan is up to in the back. I pick up the backpack and the school's keyboard harmonica that Jordan has left on the ground and head into the house. After putting Jordan's things away, I look out the kitchen window and see him lying with his belly straddling the swing seat, pushing himself back and forth with his hands. It looks terribly uncomfortable, but he is laughing up a storm so I guess he's not in too much pain.

As I would do on many occasions during that fall, I let him have a few minutes in the yard to be by himself. We learn over time that he is 100 percent reliable to stay within the area of the backyard, even though there is no fence. A short time later, I'm out with him, pushing him on the swing and trying to convince him to go for a walk. It isn't too long before I gain his consent, and we're off on the mile and a half route that we follow on all but the most inclement of days. Once we are moving, I begin to direct a steady stream of prattle Jordan's way, operating—as I had done over much of the past three years—on the principle of William The Silent that, "It isn't necessary to hope to persevere." I have seen almost no evidence over that time that any of my words are understood, nor has Jordan shown any inclination to repeat or otherwise respond to any of what I have said. I am therefore immensely surprised when he begins blowing through his teeth to make the "s" sound after I point out that he is holding a "sssssstick." In fact, I can hardly hold my joy to publicly acceptable levels as Jordan then makes the sound on his own while a jogger passes by. Heartened by this success, I begin over-emphasizing the initial sound of other objects that he shows interest in during the walk, such as leaves, mailbox, and water. To my delight, he makes an honest effort to reproduce these sounds and has some measure of success in doing so.

These sudden and fairly substantial changes in Jordan might be resulting from a number of individual factors or a combination thereof. When not reveling in his progress, Jill and I spend a considerable amount of time speculating about its cause. The most obvious explanation would be that Jordan is improving because he is now aware that he is living at home. This interpretation would account for the fact that he didn't show any signs of improving during the summer. But there are other, just as plausible, reasons, the most likely of which being that immediately prior to our coming to Massachusetts we began to give him a megavitamin supplement.

For several years we had toyed with the idea of trying these vitamins, but had been basically dissuaded by the arguments suggesting that there was little evidence of their efficacy and that big doses might be toxic to his system. We finally decided to go ahead with a trial run, primarily because of Bernard Rimland's consistent report of the effectiveness of vitamins. We also felt less concerned about negative side effects after reading Rimland's "Form Letter Regarding High Dosage Vitamin B6 and Magnesium Therapy for Autism and Related Disorders." It seemed, too, that there was little danger

in trying this experiment, since we felt confident that any
negative changes in Jordan's health or behavior would be
readily apparent to us now that he was living at home.
Rimland's form letter suggests using a megavitamin called
Super Nu-Thera manufactured by Kirkman Laboratories. A
dosage of six capsules a day is recommended for someone of
Jordan's weight. This provides 500 mg of Vitamin B6, 250 mg
of magnesium, and a host of other essential vitamins and
minerals. After a brief period of time using a lesser dosage, we
put Jordan on the recommended dosage.

Jordan's reformation could definitely be correlated with
the onset of the vitamin intake. But there are other factors
which might be playing a part as well. Maybe, for instance,
the combination of the structured Higashi school day and the
semi-structured after-school time at home affords him the best
of both worlds; or maybe it just took more than the seven
weeks at home for him to get used to the routines of our
house; or maybe the change in the weather lies at the heart of
his improvement.

Whatever the reason, his getting somewhat better comes
at a critical time, for his continued stagnation could well have
pushed us over the edge. But now that his development is
showing signs of life, we are faced with the more pleasant
dilemma of trying to determine how we can build on what he
has started. We know that Jordan, like other autistic children,
functions best in a predictable environment, heavy on
routine. But we also know that growth can only proceed if he
is given opportunities to have new experiences. Especially in
those first months, from September to December, we try to establish a daily framework of repeated activities, supplemented
with a variety of additional activities that differ from day to
day. The constants include a one-and-a-half to two-mile walk
around the neighborhood, which, after my breakthrough ex-

perience in October, doubles as a language lesson, a homework session of not less than half an hour, a ten-minute period when he plays the keyboard under our direction, and at least one chore a day. The supplements include trips to restaurants and stores, swimming, bike riding, roller skating, hiking, and some form of art activity.

The everyday activities that we select for Jordan are essentially culled from the Higashi curriculum. We have seen the benefits of daily exercise on his eating and sleeping patterns, and we want to make sure that this component, though stressed at the school itself every day, is routinized at home as well. The most readily accepted form of exercise for Jordan is walking, so this is the vehicle we choose. Again, walking has the added advantage of affording opportunities for language development in a way that is consistent with the "functional language" emphasis of the school. In this regard, Higashi stresses that language instruction should be carried out in familiar places and within the bounds of typical conversation. Thus, as we walk along, we try to point out the things in which he shows interest, and repeat, repeat, repeat. Our daily session with the keyboard is another activity which appears to enhance language development, at least in terms of sound production. The Higashi program is doing a similar type of lesson with a keyboard into which Jordan blows. Repetition is critical in this area, too, so I start off each session by having him go up and down the scale. As he touches each note, I exaggerate my mouth shape and try to entice him to make the sound. After doing this routine for about six weeks, Jordan begins to sing the notes on his own: not clearly or consistently, but definitely in imitation of me. As we continue with this process, he improves in his ability to reproduce the scale, and, in a very primitive manner, he starts singing some songs. It is merely rote singing, but it is an encouraging start. He even begins to show an awareness of rhythm and tune, sometimes laughing if he strikes the wrong note on the keyboard.

The daily routine of participating in household chores such as putting away laundry, loading and unloading the dishwasher, and clearing the table after meals also generates positive effects. For example, when we first start making these activities part of his everyday experience, Jordan is extremely reluctant to participate, walking abruptly out of the kitchen or laundry room as soon as he realizes what we're asking him to do. But, over time, he not only begins to accept the responsibility, he also exhibits greater organization in carrying out the tasks. Better still, he begins to regain the ability to categorize—a simple cognitive skill he hasn't shown in almost three years. The concept finally reemerges in October of 1989 with his learning how to place the knives, forks, and spoons in the appropriate slots of the silverware tray.

Even the supplemental activities, which were initially viewed merely as a way to fill up the day, have a positive impact. Prior to the move, we had pretty much decided that physical activities would be the primary way of rounding out Jordan's schedule. He has always had fairly close to normal coordination, and has seemed to enjoy such activities, so we anticipated that doing things like swimming and roller skating would be a pretty positive way of passing the time. What we didn't expect, however, was how much he would improve in these activities, and how improvements in this area would help him to become more organized in general.

There are many moments from the months of October and November of 1989 which are memorable in this regard. Some of them occur at Concord's "Thoreau Club," where Jordan first learns to dive to the bottom of the pool to retrieve a sunken object; where he first swims the length of the pool; and where he has his first exposure to a hot tub. And I can recall similar firsts at the roller rink in Hudson and the YMCA in Framingham.

The most exciting of these experiences, however, comes during a visit from my mother in mid-November. For several weeks before her visit, we had been taking Jordan out to the street with his bike to acquaint him with riding in an area with traffic. Due to the steepness of the streets, we had only ridden around the track in Maryland. But we wanted him to be aware of the dangers of the road before he actually learned how to ride, so our lessons occur there.

The first few sessions without the training wheels are maddening, because even though Jordan needs to make only some minor adjustments to take off and fly, he can't understand our directions. And because he has gotten used to having the support of the training wheels, it comes as quite an affront to him that he is crashing. Not to mention that he is getting pretty banged up in the process. On the second day of my mother's visit, I come up with the idea that if Jill and I run on either side of him while Mom watches Leslie, he might intuit what needs to be done to stay perpendicular.

On the very first try, it works. He's halfway up the road, on his own, in no time at all. And in his happy giggling and squealing I see how pleased he is with himself. Just as when he learned to swim, he seems to understand that this is an accomplishment; that he has joined some kind of club. And we're all beside ourselves with joy. Even Leslie's eyes widen as she watches him pedal along and shouts, "Goooood boy, Jordan!" in encouragement. When the short ride is over, Jordan briefly dashes away from the bike, but comes right back to it with a big smile on his face and grabs the handlebars to show he wants another ride.

On Thanksgiving Day, there is an eight-inch snowfall in Boston, and in December the weather turns bitterly cold. The snow stays on the ground well into January before there is a brief thaw followed by more snow. Now there is no bike riding; walking and running are difficult; our stays outside are shorter; and Jordan begins another period of downturn.

It was in December of 1984 that we first learned that Jordan had autism: it was in December of 1985 that we became so frustrated with Jordan's progress in the public school system that we decided to abandon that education for the "Option" alternative: and now, in December, 1989, the light of day is short again.

Once more Jordan is resisting public places and balking at participating in organized activities. Once again he is irritable and prone to unprovoked outbursts. And, most discouraging of all, his development seems once more to have leveled off.

The lowest moments come during the second week of December, while Jill and Leslie are away on their third monthly trip to Maryland. During their first two visits, I had basically positive experiences. Even on the long weekends, I found enough to do to keep Jordan busy and reasonably well-focused and to make the time pass quickly and productively. In fact, it was a genuine source of gratification to have handled these situations with a minimum of frustration; my self-esteem and confidence rising with each of Jordan's steps forward; my endorphin production again registering in the "sad-normal" range. As I have not yet learned to become detached from results, however, this latest regression makes it especially hard to cope. If I remember that mid-November day when Jordan made his first unassisted bike ride with particular fondness, I need go no further than a month later to remember a day that produces its emotional antithesis. As on so many days during that bleak December, I am bucking a frigid wind when I sprint out to meet the special education wagon as Jordan arrives home. As I open the car door and unleash a blast of polar air into the front seat, Jordan shrinks away and looks as if he is about to kick me for suggesting that his comfortably heated ride is over. A minor scuffle ensues, but I finally get him out of the car and racing toward the house.

Once in the house, he settles down a bit, and even appears to forgive me when I offer him some juice and a snack. Normally, he wouldn't get any food at this hour, but I'm interested in cultivating a little goodwill in order that I might coax him into going outside again for a ride to the pool. We aren't going to be able to get any other form of exercise on a day like this, and there's only so much you can do inside all evening with an autistic child. Usually, this situation presents no problem: Jordan likes the water and has had nothing but good experiences since we began taking him to the swim club over two months ago. The entire family has enjoyed our trips to this club, because the water is almost always very comfortable, the staff is accommodating and understanding of Jordan, and we have met a number of very nice people there. It is the one place in Massachusetts that we've been to more than a handful of times where Jordan has never protested.

This trip to the club starts out no different than any other. Jordan willingly takes his bathing suit and a change of clothes out of his dresser, puts on his coat and heads out to the car. There is no telltale whining when we pull into the parking lot, and he tractably follows directions to gather his things and close the car door once we've stopped. He is stable and restrained even as we enter the building.

But after checking in at the front desk, he catches a glimpse of the pool as we head down the steps to the locker room. Perhaps noticing two boys laughing and splashing in the pool, he begins a deliberate approach toward the glass door. Having no idea how determined he is to enter the pool area without going through the formality of putting on his bathing suit, I suggest in a soft voice that we stop off in the locker room first. Though my comment is the gentlest sort of entreaty, one would have thought it the command of a drill sergeant judging from Jordan's reaction. After hearing my words, his face gets flushed, and he charges me, almost knocking me down the steps. When I hold my hand out in self-defense, he rushes past me in a headlong sprint into a nearby wall. His body obeys the law of physics having to do with equal and opposite reactions, and he falls into a crumpled heap after a spectacular crash.

Upon determining that he's not hurt—just mad—I try to imagine the thoughts of the few witnesses to the incident. But I don't get too big a window for contemplation, as Jordan begins to repeatedly strike my body with his fists. I'm too flustered to develop a negotiating strategy, so simply and softly I suggest that we leave. We backtrack past the receptionist's desk, our incandescent faces casting a glaring light of embarrassment and rage.

The shock and adrenalin flow associated with this incident gradually settle down into a numbed silence under the calming effect of the car ride. It is only a matter of minutes before Jordan appears to have forgotten what happened. It makes me wonder how his mind represents the events of his life. If only I could understand the mechanisms by which he interprets his environment, how much better could I make things for him. At this moment, in the Acton shopping center parking lot, I am stricken by a revelation. Autism—at least as it is manifested in Jordan—can best be described as the antipode of what historian Thomas Berry has suggested are the fundamental processes of the universe: differentiation, complexity, and connectedness. Against this mainstream Jordan clings to his sameness, simplicity, and isolation. Like some flammable, inert gas he cannot be made to combine, and he must be handled with care. His moments of tranquility can be shattered at any time, like when the simplicity and sameness of a car ride in the dark threatens to be interrupted by a trip into the grocery store. If, as happens in this instance, there is something subtly different about the way I stop the car, or the manner in which I ask him to open or close the door, there could be an eruption. Recognizing now some such difference between this and other recent trips to the grocery store which have occurred without incident, Jordan kicks the dashboard and begins twisting violently in the seatbelt as the car comes to a stop. No use kidding myself about this venture: I might as well turn around and go home. It is only six o'clock when we pull into the driveway. Another three hours till bed.

At least when we're home, Jordan doesn't seem as agitated as he was during the first part of the evening. He is, however, anxious to see some progress on dinner, so I hurry up a meal of fish sticks, frozen spinach, and an apple; all of which takes him less than five minutes to eat. There's still quite a bit of time left, and, on a night when everything has gone so poorly, I have to fight my inclination to allow him to vegetate the rest of his waking time. But I'm not terribly confident about his reaction to the menu of activities that typically comes in this time slot. I know in advance, for example, that the sight of the school's prescribed homework (tracing words from a story the class has heard) will not elicit peals of joy. But I know, too, that, on most nights, the struggle to have him participate is preferable to the dull pain I can get from watching him spin his cocoon of self-stimulation.

I decide to break away from the pattern of homework after eating, and opt, instead, for something that I know will be well received—tickling. Around the circle that passes through our living room, dining room, and kitchen, I chase after Jordan. Every twenty steps or so he stops and throws his arms straight into the air to indicate that he wants to be tickled under the arms. When I comply, he falls in a giggling heap on the floor, then, after a while, he's up and running to start the game all over again. We go round and round like this for about fifteen minutes before he reaches his saturation point.

Afterwards, watching him pick up toys and tap them on various surfaces, I consider how soliciting tickling is Jordan's only form of self-initiated social interaction. If left to his own devices, this would be the only thing, aside from food and water, for which Jordan would engage others. All other forms of contact must be imposed. What an awesome craving for sameness!

The tapping stops: Jordan has to go to the bathroom. I follow him in, thinking that I may as well get his nightly bath in at this time, since he rarely refuses this activity once he's already in the bathroom. When his clothes are off, I turn on the water. "Look, Jordan, what's this?" I ask, scooping up a handful of the water. "Waa," he responds in a drawn-out fashion. "Good boy: you're learning your words. It's good to talk. Soon you'll be able to tell people what you want." The praise is left untouched by acknowledgment.

I bend over to the sink behind me to pick up several bath toys with which Jordan has recently been "playing." Included in the collection are a small plastic ball, a cup, a plastic man, and a car. For lack of anything better to do during bathtime, I have been working on getting him to identify and say the names of these toys. In the past week or so, I have begun to form the opinion that he might be understanding the words which represent the objects. He hasn't proven this yet by identifying each object that I ask him to touch with 100 percent accuracy, but he has been doing better than one would expect from chance. His pattern of responding in these informal assessments is, in fact, quite odd, both in its inconsistency and in its indication that he may be able to say (in rough fashion) the names of objects which he can't pick out in a group.

Tonight is exemplary of this pattern and of how the frustration of witnessing it can lead to regrettable behavior on my part. After finishing the washing part of Jordan's bath, I line up the four objects along the edge of the tub. "Jordan," I say, picking up the toy man and zooming it past his head. "What's this?" "Maaa," he responds, showing the faintest hint of a smile as I pat him on the head in encouragement. The same sequence is repeated with the other objects, and, for three of them, he makes the correct first syllable, giving the appearance, since three correct responses is two more than the number that would have been expected from pure guessing, that he understands what he's doing. On a repeat trial, however, he gets only two correct. And when I ask him to touch the object that I say, he fails to identify any. Though I've seen this kind of performance maybe thirty times, tonight it seems incomprehensible to me. So I go through the process again, and I raise my voice way out of line when he can't pick out the object any better on the second trial. "No, Jordan, I want the man!"

The words are hardly out of my mouth when he begins to emit a soft crying sound. Like any normal child, he's showing shame and fear at my stupid outburst. Now I'm crying too. And apologizing. I put my arm around him as he comes out of the bath and drape him with a towel. Somewhat later, in the darkened dining room, Jordan and I bring our separate closures to this horrible evening under blankets and the still and unrevealing gaze of the Big Dipper, peering in through the sliding-glass door.

VI

A string of warm days has poked a welcome-mat-sized hole in the snow covering the entrance to Acton's Spring Hill conservation area. Jordan employs the good footing at this spot like a starting block to help him build a big lead on me down the trail. Even before I'm out of the car, he's thirty yards ahead, giving no thought to his father or the car door he has left open in his wake.

It's Saturday afternoon, and I'm amazed that he has this kind of energy after having spent the better portion of his morning doing vigorous physical exercises at Higashi. But, then again, he's always had sufficient stamina for the things he enjoys, even tackling a tough 2.75 mile trail like this. At least today I won't have to run to keep up with him, the snow having made the trail too treacherous to negotiate at Jordan's usual pace. And it's good that our speed will be more deliberate, for my mind is a pocketful of thoughts, images, and issues which I want to consider as we travel.

I have spent the balance of my morning in another fruit-less search for consensus with Jill about what we should do in the coming year, so images and thoughts of this dialogue are the first things my mind empties from its pocket as I move. It seems we are dug into our positions; Jill steadfastly holding to her belief that only Higashi can properly educate Jordan; I wondering whether he might not be better served in a program that emphasizes communication. At this point, I'm also again raising the issue of financial security. It's clear by this time (late January, 1990) that the Massachusetts economy is in free fall, and that the "education industry" will be hard hit. And, I'm no longer even confident that Jill will be able to find comparable work, despite her protestations to the contrary. Ultimately, the argument hinges on the "all other things being equal" factor. For my part, I no longer believe that Higashi will bring Jordan to a level beyond what would be expected from any structured program. It's not so much the recent regression which makes me feel this way (actually, by this time, he has again become manageable, and his mood has gotten better). Rather, it is my sense that the behavioral improvements and the foundation skills that the school has established would not be jeopardized by a change of programs, and my further belief that Jordan's cognitive functioning sets basic limits which I feel other programs would also be able to attain.

But Jill's position remains solid; that leaving Higashi might precipitate serious regression; and that no other program could handle Jordan as a day student. Additionally, she feels there are many advantages in Massachusetts that make it the venue of choice even if she agreed to the argument that everything else was equal. Included among these advantages are her preference for the living conditions of Massachusetts, its proximity to a core of people with autistic children who are good advocates and who serve as a built-in support group, and the fact that the Massachusetts special education officials seem more client-centered.

After we have laid out and dissected our positions, we are left with the "either or" nature of our decision, which makes compromise seem impossible. It is at this juncture that Jill introduces the notion that what is needed is for me to find work in Massachusetts. She remains convinced that, if I were more aggressive, I could find satisfying employ at a level of pay reasonably close to what I made in Baltimore. My experience over the first three months in Boston seems to contradict this, though. During that period, I've submitted a dozen or so resumes in response to advertized positions and have not even been granted an interview in return. As I frequently remind Jill, public education is often a closed business where the practice of hiring from within generally freezes out those attempting to make lateral moves from other systems in all but the highest positions. Private education is an alternative, but the low pay and the lack of benefits make it a hard choice. And, I'm further limited by the fact that Jill herself has not set roots down in Massachusetts; thus any work that I got would have to be sufficiently flexible as to allow me to arrive late and leave early during those days in which she was in Maryland.

The possibility is raised by Jill and others that I might take a part-time position at a community college in hopes of turning it into a full-time job later on. But later, when such an opportunity actually occurs, my resume again fails to attract a response.

All of this talk of alternatives fails to address an issue that has troubled me since I've been in Massachusetts; namely that in leaving my position in Baltimore I'll be giving up an opportunity to make a significant contribution. Jill rudely dismisses this thought, reminding me at every chance how I did nothing but complain about my situation when I was there. Nonetheless, immediately before I left, I had begun to feel that my recent association with an innovative federally funded project headed by a renowned educational researcher—Bob Slavin of Johns Hopkins University—might enable me to make a real difference. Furthermore, articles I had been writing on urban education were just starting to get published in the *Baltimore Sun*, and I felt that this was an avenue of influence which had only begun to be tapped.

I'm at the trail's first landmark—a foot bridge about three quarters of a mile into the hike—before my thoughts return to earth. "Wow, Jordan, what a good hiker you are! We're already at the bridge!" I shout at his back as he begins to race across the bridge, still holding to his substantial lead. My words cause him to stop and look back, and the abrupt pause triggers his fall off the narrow bridge. He laughs at himself, perhaps realizing that had he done this in any other season, he would have taken a bath along with the fall. Today, though, he just lands on the slab of ice covering the stream.

Only seconds after we have left the bridge, Jordan is foraging around in the snow, looking for the thing that will complete his ideal environment—a tapping stick. He pulls hard on some young trees, and tramples a few ground pines before he notices a twig of the correct dimensions under a log that is blocking the path. He bends down to get the stick and starts tapping it against the log, presumably to insure that it conforms to his standards in such matters. When it is obvious that it meets the test, Jordan is off again, stomping and tapping down the path.

Observing this little vignette calls forth the next thought from the disarrayed collection lying dormant in my brain. It is an idea which Jill has stressed for months and one that I have come close to accepting through my reading about Buddhism and, more recently, in my viewing of the PBS series "The Power of Myth." In this brilliant dialogue with Bill Moyers, mythology scholar Joseph Campbell repeatedly emphasizes that humanity's essentially common mythology expresses the elementary idea that an invisible plane supports what we see here on earth. A derivative theme of this idea is that we are best served by living in the present. Somehow, seeing this funny episode of Jordan's stick fetish brings the beauty of living in the here and now into focus. In this beautiful and ancient woods, an autistic boy taps out his existential statement with a stick. Along with the trees and the snow and the current flowing under the sheet of ice beneath my feet, I am in this moment, unfolding. We are deep in the woods now, about halfway around the trail, passing through a grove of birch trees with their white trunks arching like shoots of snow from a pale and frozen soil. At this time of year, the sun penetrates the trail enough so that the trunks of the birches are lightly painted with the final glimmering rays of daylight as we travel through. All of this natural beauty brings to mind the native Americans who haunted this place centuries ago. On a day like today I can see how it might have been that being immersed in nature is what led them to the belief that all that lives is holy. It leaves a body incredulous that in a handful of generations this landscape came to be dominated by people with an entirely different philosophy.

Being an inheritor of that latter tradition has had a profound effect on how I view the world, and, obviously, this would include my reaction to having a child like Jordan. I am so accustomed to dividing experience into its sacred and profane piles that it seems natural to think of Jordan as deficient; to think of his life as meaningless. But this characterization notwithstanding, he is no less alive. And in the grand scheme of things his existence is no less meaningful than anyone else's.

It is true that he is fundamentally different from the norm in being unable to apply verbal overtones to his experience; but despite this handicap, he still interprets and reacts to that experience on some level. And though he may always lack the ability to communicate, this in itself would not prohibit him from developing a certain awareness of his environment and an appreciation for his life. I must recognize that my disappointment and periodic sadness about Jordan reflect back on me. It is I who am deficient for cursing the hand that I've been dealt; for yearning for the perks of parenthood; for not accepting Jordan as he is.

So much ruminating has diminished my sense of time. Fortunately, with darkness rapidly descending, we reach the end of the path. ❄

❄

❄

❄

❄ When the one-time great player and part-time philosopher of baseball, Yogi Berra, used to say that, "It ain't over till it's over," he might well have had the New England winter in mind. Here, in late March, Jordan, my father-in-law, and I, all bundled up, are tromping on the still hard ground of Acton's partially frozen Nagog Hill trail. With Jordan, as usual, well ahead of us, I'm pouring the most recent distillation of my thoughts into the ever-willing ears of one of the most patient men in the universe. During the nearly twenty years that I've known him, Kabe has had to endure more than his share of parenting ordeals, and yet through it all he has maintained equanimity. I'm taking advantage of that pleasant attribute again today as I try to win him over to my position in the long-standing debate over what Jill and I should do with the rest of our lives.

"I can't understand it, Kabe," I begin. "You know as well as I do that Jordan has gotten about all he's going to get out of the Higashi program. It just doesn't matter anymore whether he's in this type of structured program or another. His speech hasn't improved; his behavior is erratic; and his functioning remains very low. Given this picture, I think it makes more sense to move back to Maryland and get our lives back in order. I think Higashi has helped Jordan. But now it's time to return to our family, friends, and careers."

Even when being serious, it seems that Kabe can't deliver a message without a smile, and now the corners of his mouth turn up slightly as he issues his reply. "You've said a couple of things that I have questions about. First, you said that Jordan would be just as well served in any kind of structured program. But you've never been able to find such a program in Maryland. The only two placements I ever heard anything about were the place with the straightjackets in the hall in D.C. and the totally unstructured program in Howard County. You're not considering these, are you?"

"No, but we were limited in our search then because Howard County didn't have an appropriate public school placement for autistic children. Places like Montgomery County do, though. And I think we would find a very different kind of program there."

Appearing somewhat satisfied with this response, Kabe pushes on with his next point: "The other issue you need to consider is that Jill feels very differently about Maryland than you do. She says that it is better for her here because she has people like the Niedermeyers she can relate to about having an autistic child."

"I have the opposite view of this, Kabe. I want autism to become less of a focus in my life. I think it would be better for both of us if we had more contact with people who didn't have an autistic child. Besides, any school where Jordan would go would have some kind of parent's support group."

Not wanting to be disagreeable, but obviously aware that I face an uphill battle in convincing Jill, Kabe shakes his head and moves on. Later on in the hike, he asks me what would happen if we moved back to Maryland and we couldn't find an acceptable placement.

"Well," I slowly reply, realizing I'm about to introduce a radical concept that will meet with a good deal of resistance, "my Plan B is to work with Jordan myself at home. I really believe, having worked with him this past year and having observed the Higashi techniques more often, that I have the confidence and will to be effective with him. I know that it would be difficult, but I think I could convince the authorities that I would do as good a job as anyone: and certainly I'd be more motivated. And there's another reason I think Plan B is worth considering, and that is that I'm not sure that there will always be legislative support for public funding of special education. Here in Massachusetts I've already seen articles outlining the financial difficulties of the public schools and how the costs of special education contribute to these woes. If hard economic times produce a big enough backlash, we might easily revert to the bad old days of 'catch as catch can' special education."

Kabe is really shaking his head now. "You could never do it."

Further discussions over the rest of Carol and Kabe's stay fail to produce any breakthrough, but, gradually, over the next month or so, I begin to realize the truth of what others are saying about Plan B. It's simply not workable. If only there was a quality program somewhere close to Baltimore, where we could feel confident that Jordan would not be permitted to spend his days in debilitating self-isolation. If there was just a program that we could trust to keep him involved and active. Or, taking the other side, if there were only positions that promised security, reasonable pay, and the potential for making a positive contribution here in Boston. At this juncture of the journey, I can empathize with the people of Eastern Europe. In early December, 1989, they were basking in the euphoria of the fallen wall and the disintegration of Communism. By April, however, they were confronting the hard realities of a degraded environment and a ruined economy.

And, as for me, in December I had seen the first four months of our stay in Massachusetts go well: and I had even begun to have a glimmer of hope that Jordan would start to communicate again. By April, though, many of Jordan's problems had resurfaced, and it seemed that the continuing uncertainty of our situation could threaten our marriage.

But when two people approach the edge of a chasm from opposite sides, one inevitable result is that they move closer to each other. And so it is with Jill and me. Before she leaves on her April trip to Maryland, I have already publicly abandoned Plan B, and she, in turn, has agreed to reopen the investigation of autism programs in Maryland. If what she finds is unacceptable, the room for negotiation will shrink precipitously, but at least I will have had the satisfaction of knowing that she was flexible enough to make the effort.

Things happen quickly in this chapter, but for all the action the end result reads, once again, like Bruce Springsteen's "One Step Forward Two Steps Back." Once in Maryland, Jill focuses her search on the Montgomery County public school program for autistic children. The reputation that precedes this program is that it has a well-structured curriculum that emphasizes communication and practical living skills. When Jill actually visits the site of the most likely placement for Jordan, she observes a program pretty much in line with that reputation. The impression that she reports to me on the phone is that the classes are run in a professional, clinical manner, by teachers who seem enthusiastic about their work. And additional conversations with administrators and parents also convey a positive sense of the program.

On the down side, the school is only in session four and a half days a week, and there isn't much of a summer component. What's more, Jordan would have a fairly long bus ride to school, and he would be receiving fewer hours of instruction in the arts and phys-ed there. Higashi also has the advantage of being a program with which Jordan is comfortable. It's a difficult call, but Jill's initial response is that Montgomery County might be acceptable.

We'll need more time to consider the ramifications of all this, but the immediate task will be for me to visit the school. If things look good to me, we can proceed with the initial paper work and begin to look for a house to rent. I can also use the time in Maryland to begin to explore the options available to me in the Baltimore public schools when I return in the fall.

By the time I make my visit to the school in the first week of May, it is almost anticlimactic. I have resolved in my heart that I will like this program unless something crazy happens. And nothing does. The teacher and the assistant work with students in groups of two or three. Specific language and cognitive objectives, such as identifying pictures, counting, or using the correct prepositional phrase, are the focus. The lessons are rapid-fire, with the teachers speaking in staccato cadences and the students being expected to respond quickly and clearly to questions and directions. It is far from inspiring, but there is a discernible method, in pursuit of clear and attainable goals. No dogs and ponies; no educationese; no straightjackets; and no pretensions to miracle working. Jordan will be all right here.

Now I allow my hopes to rise for a peaceful solution to our dilemma, and I prepare to put the tensions and uncertainties behind us. When I go to sleep that night I think of the possibilities of once again being able to focus on enjoying Jordan, Leslie, and Jill, and on having a life outside of autism.

I should know better by now, but I don't. Though sources from religion to mythology to the events in my own life have been my constant instructors, I have yet to internalize life's most fundamental lesson—as long as you are motivated by fears or desires, you will have no peace. Only when you become detached from expectations, can the manic-depressive cycle be avoided. And this can't be learned didactically, you must be shaken again and again until the idea settles like dust on your soul. It is a continuous process of self-education against the natural inclination to believe that life will take a predictable and happy course. ✳

✳

✳

✳

✳ For two weeks I've been tied to the expectation that I'll soon be living a more settled life. But all of that changes when, during her May visit to Maryland, Jill learns that Jordan is not guaranteed a spot in the program that she observed. We are not yet residents of Montgomery County, and it is possible that the limited number of slots will be filled by the time Jordan's placement is considered. The special education officials who pass on this new information are all assurances that an appropriate alternative can be found, but the knowledge of this potentiality leaves Jill worried enough to start resurrecting old concerns. The lack of phys-ed, art, and music; the anxiety-provoking nature of intense one-on-one instruction; the reduced school day; and the complex child-care arrangements that would have to be made if we opted for this program—all of this begins to pile up like poorly stacked blocks. Pretty soon the whole idea is crashing to the floor.

Having invested a considerable effort in reestablishing old ties with former colleagues in the Baltimore public school system, I'm a little miffed at the idea of abandoning our plan to return so quickly, but, on the other hand, I can appreciate Jill's thinking. It's just wearying to be continuously jerked around like this. And we also have the stressor of having very little time to actually decide for sure what we'll be doing come September. If we're staying in Massachusetts—and everything would point in that direction now—then I have to get cracking about a job search. Jill, too, will have to make some arrangements. Unless I get a reasonable paying position, she'll have to ask Maryland for another year's extension of her current situation. And, if she does that, any kind of employment that I get will have to be flexible enough to allow me to come in late and leave early about a third of the time—a very unlikely proposition in the field of education. Furthermore, things have only gotten worse in the Boston area over the past few months, and there isn't much room for optimism. So what I think I'm seeing is the prospect of choosing between underemployment and a second hole in my resume.

As Jordan's school year comes to a close, I begin to sense a softening of Jill's position. Maybe she's just concerned about my mental health, or maybe she has accepted my argument that if I become underemployed or fail to find work I may have to retrain entirely. Under any other circumstances, retraining would not be so bad: people are forced to do it all the time, obviously. But with full-time responsibility for Jordan there simply isn't time; especially with Jill so often out-of-state. With less than a month left before I must notify Baltimore of my intentions for the coming year, Jill agrees that, if I can find no suitable work in Massachusetts, we'll go back home.

For having won the battle, so to speak, I am, nonetheless, no less worried that Jill is about going home to an uncertain placement for Jordan. Jaded as I am, I still don't believe that Jordan's schooling doesn't matter. If he gets put in a program that is damaging, there will be more lost than a career: he could turn aggressive or self-abusive. But, still, I am relieved that we have a fallback position, for I can't possibly imagine anything turning up in the short period of time before the deadline.

Just when my expectations are lowest, serendipity appears, offering the maxim, "Don't ask, and it shall be given. Don't seek, and you shall find." For several months I have been working with Boston Higashi's Director of Development as a member of a fundraising committee. Because I had experience as a grant writer, she thought that I might be of assistance to the school in this capacity. During this period, we have developed a good relationship, and, after she decides to leave her post in June, the idea of my assuming her position gets kicked around. Since there is no clear indication from the school that they are even planning to continue the position, all of the talk is just speculation. Indeed, it isn't until the first week of July that the principal decides to interview me.

For both of us, the interview is a new experience. Being new to this American post, it's the first time he has had to interview a foreigner: and, for me, it's the first time I've required a translator in such a situation. As I answer the questions, I wonder whether what I'm saying is being accurately interpreted; whether he can get a sense from what he's hearing about my ability to do the job; and how he can get a feel for the intangibles that generally play such a critical role in evaluating a prospective employee.

The principal is facing all these uncertainties and others as well, including, again, whether the school should have such a position (the other people who have held the job haven't been all that successful in raising money), whether it should be full- or part-time, and whether to trust a parent with the kinds of sensitive information that a person holding such a position would be privy to. And now that he has initiated the process of considering me for the job, the principal must also think about how rejecting my candidacy might affect parental support. Since many of the parents know that I'm a candidate for the job, and some are also aware that I will probably leave the area if I don't get it, there may be some dissatisfaction expressed if I'm not given a shot.

And if arriving at a decision will be difficult for the school's administration, it will be even more so for us, as we have considerably more at stake. I have to think, for starters, whether I can live with what, at least for next year, will surely be a part-time offer. Related to this will be the question of whether I can obtain health insurance benefits and what restrictions will be placed on me in getting other kinds of part time work, should I need to supplement my income. I must also consider the pros and cons of entering a field in which I'm only marginally qualified, not only for my own sake, but for the school's as well. The issue of salary is another concern, especially when Jill leaves her job. And, finally, after months of thinking about how I should be making autism less a focus of my personal life, I have to ask myself if I really want it to extend to my work life too.

In the final week before I must notify Baltimore of my intentions for the coming year, I receive a call from the principal's interpreter with an offer of two days a week at a salary that strikes me as being more appropriate for one. It's the kind of beginning which almost shuts down the process immediately, but Jill has her heart set on making this thing work, so there will be no quitting without making a counter offer. Several more rounds are required, however, before we come to a position which is even remotely close to being agreeable. My initial inclination is to reject the final offer and go home, but I know by now that if I do that I'll be doing it alone. No, if I pull out my oar and jump ship, I'll drown; and, without me, Jill will paddle around in circles. Another adventure is underway—in a new language.

Immediately after accepting the school's offer, two very reassuring things happen. First, Baltimore agrees to extend my leave of absence for another year, thus allowing me the luxury of seeing how things go at Higashi; and, second, many of the parents at the school go out of their way to offer encouragement and support for my decision. The combination of these circumstances makes me feel both confident and secure that everything will work out one way or another.

Around the middle of July, we come to terms on the deal, which calls for me to work four days a week at a salary substantially, but not unconscionably, lower than what I'd be making if I'd gone back to Baltimore. The principal doesn't want me to begin working until the start of the school year in September, but this arrangement suits us fine, too, as we have daily responsibility for Jordan for all but two weeks in that period anyway.

Except for a brief interlude in Maryland, we spend the entire summer in Massachusetts, and during that time we get to know our new friends, the Niedermeyers, particularly well, sharing many a Sunday afternoon together at the Salisbury State Park on the coast. On those hot July and August days we'd watch their son, Sam, lope out into the ocean to depths over his head with Ben trailing, fighting the undertow and the increasing strength of his boy, to keep him from drowning. And while his classmate headed due east whenever he hit the beach, Jordan would do all of his traveling north and south, sometimes getting as far as a mile away, giggling, flapping his arms, and splashing in puddles as he ran along the shore line; never getting into the water above his knees.

The camaraderie of these outings makes me realize for the first time the potential for developing special relationships with other members of families with handicapped children, once the pain of having such a child begins to subside. Even after one has become accustomed to the experience, so much of the day-to-day life with an autistic child can seem like purgatory: but developing this kind of soul-mate friendship crystallizes the meaning of Dante's vision that the love of God informs the universe even to the depths of hell. It has been almost five years since we have had such comfortable fellowship with another family over an extended period of time; and this lack of a familial friendship seems, in retrospect, to have been one of the worst elements of our ordeal. Our friendship with the Niedermeyers also represents the first time since we've known Jordan was autistic that we have felt appreciated for what we could bring to a friendship. During our get togethers, I am, at times, reminded of all the isolation that Jill and I felt during those initial months—no, years—when even our friends and relatives became estranged from us because of our special circumstance. Looking back on that long period of disconnectedness, brings home very clearly how having this kind of a relationship may be the sine qua non of mental health; and, given the rarity and unyielding nature of the disorder, it is easy to understand why so many parents of autistic children are chronically depressed. For the opportunity to find others with whom you can give and obtain counsel may never present itself.

Though Sunday afternoons are consistently fun during the seven-week vacation, the rest of the summer is grueling. For us, there is at least a brief summer camp period provided by our community; the Niedermeyers aren't so lucky. After only two days, Sam is kicked out of the camp in which he was to participate. This is a devastating blow for Ben and Joanne, as it means they must have Sam all day. And since Ben is working full time, the onus of caring for Sam falls on Joanne. We try to provide her with some respite by taking Sam on several occasions, but it isn't long before we have Jordan all day and can't make a further commitment.

Being alone with Sam gives Jill and me the opportunity to experience the living proof of one of those childhood adages which almost never rang true. Remember when you were particularly depressed as a child, and somebody—usually one of your parents—said, "Cheer up, there's always somebody who has it worse than you?" The combination of a hot July afternoon and a three-hour shift with Sam Niedermeyer convinces me of the truth of that old aphorism. To put it gently, Sam is wired. Unless held or trapped in a corner, he is constantly on the move: climbing up on counters; getting into cabinets; opening the refrigerator and spilling its contents; putting any and everything into his mouth. Your free time is measured in nano-seconds, the potential for danger is constant. Outside, the challenges don't disappear, they just change. When not restrained, Sam is instantaneously out into the street, heedless of traffic. At a playground, he is performing death-defying acts on the top of the tallest equipment. In public places . . . forget it.

This is a child whose father celebrated Christmas in Boston's Logan Airport because it was the only large indoor facility that was open. Though spending time with Sam Niedermeyer makes us appreciate the progress that Jordan has made, it doesn't make the day-to-day challenges of August any less trying. And our normal difficulties with this period are compounded by the new compulsions he begins manifesting at this time. On particularly hot days, for example, we would allow him to use an ice pick to break chunks of ice out of an ice tray. Initially, this seemed like a reasonably purposeful activity that might even enhance his powers of concentration. By the end of the summer, however, he is opening up the freezer every time he comes into the kitchen and tantrumming whenever he isn't allowed to "pick."

The tantrums themselves begin to take on a more compulsive quality during this period as well. Heretofore, he might swing his arms or stamp his feet or do any of the typical things that accompany a small child's fit of anger. Now, though, his emotional outbursts begin to be highlighted by acts of self-injury and aggression centering on his own and other's hands. Usually in these episodes he takes either his ring or pinky finger and bends it back to the base of his knuckles. If we try to ignore this self-mutilation, he works even harder to get our attention, sometimes by attacking us and attempting to wreak havoc on our fingers.

Other fetishes which emerge at this time include tilting back the chair he is sitting in, manifesting anger whenever someone cracks his knuckles (something I do almost unconsciously and with great frequency), and closing all open doors. Interruption or, in the case of the knuckle cracking, initiation, of any of these acts can often precipitate finger mutilation; so this new behavior is especially troubling. We are not only concerned about what he might be doing to the muscles in his hands, but also that the self-injury and compulsive nature of his behavior might escalate. Worse, these new problems don't seem to improve when Jordan returns to Higashi in the fall, as generally happens when he regresses over the summer.

It's particularly discouraging for Jill since she has to spend more time with him now that I'm working full time. She, in fact, is totally responsible for both Leslie and Jordan during the two times of day that he is at his worst, right before he leaves for school and just after he gets home. One harried Oc-

tober morning plucked from my memory is exemplary of many
others in this period.

   At 6:40 I've just returned from my morning run. It is an
unusually warm day, so I'm thoroughly soaked when I get into
the house. Not wanting to drip sweat all over the place, I take
off my clothes in the laundry room and dry myself with a dirty
towel hanging over the hamper. Naked, but dry, I climb the
stairs leading up to the living room. The house is quiet but for
the low murmur Jordan often emits after he wakes. It is an
hour before he leaves for school. Because he typically doesn't
fall asleep until 10:00, we usually let him stay in bed until
about forty-five minutes before he must leave. Jill is taking advantage of the last few minutes before the onset of Armaged-
don, sipping coffee and looking at the paper. She gives me a
little smile as I rush by on the way to the shower.

   By the time I finish my shower, the battle has begun. I
hear loud crying coming from Jordan's room and the steady
repetition of Jill's command, "Put your clothes on, Jordan.
Come on, get up. It's time for breakfast." Jill is a weary and increasingly testy drill sergeant; the recruits are in for trouble.
While getting dressed in our bedroom, I catch phase two of
the confrontation. "Stop that, Jordan. Don't do that to your
fingers!" Jill resolutely implores. As on a number of prior occasions when this behavior has presented itself, I feel compelled to intervene in the encounter. Not that my urge to
help out in these situations ever helps; quite the contrary,
when Jordan sees me coming, he mangles his fingers even
more. And when I try to pry them apart, he applies his surprisingly strong grip to my own fingers. After I get myself free, Jordan makes a kind of charge at me, to which I respond with a
business-like shove that sends him tumbling to the floor. This
is incomprehensible; a morning wrestling match with my
eight-year-old child.

The balance of the breakfast proceeds in similar fashion with Jordan exhibiting this self-injurious and aggressive behavior almost the entire time. He doesn't even eat his breakfast. When Betty finally arrives to take Jordan to school, we're near tears and totally drained. "This can't go on, Craig," Jill says in a soft voice. Nodding my head, I turn to see Leslie standing quietly in the doorway to the kitchen. I ask myself how much of this gets to her as I give them both energy-less hugs on the way out the door.

Jordan's period of severe tantrums, self-abuse, and aggression lasts about eight weeks. Over that time we employ a variety of strategies, some planned, some on impulse. Nothing we do, however, seems to have much of an impact. When he moves out of this phase it appears to happen almost overnight. Over the course of several days, he goes from a fairly consistent pattern of from four to six incidents a day to an equally consistent pattern of two or fewer occurrences. I wish that I could tell other families undergoing similar experiences the magic formula which precipitated this dramatic turn around, but, alas, nothing comes to mind. Many things were tried, including proactive ignoring, counter aggression, modified versions of holding therapy, distracting commands, and other methods too numerous to mention. None with any measurable effect. The answer seemed to be time.

Having had this dark hour with Jordan, we are now aware that there are substantial limitations to what we can know about him. Throughout this period, we could identify no definite cause of his malcontent, and we were equally unable to find a cure. It's a sobering aspect of our lives that brings us back to the reality that putting out visions of a future for Jordan is risky business, even if that future calls for nothing more than his being able to live with us. But undergoing conflict, as Heraclitus once suggested, can also facilitate growth. If we must give up our complacency about Jordan never becoming self-abusive or aggressive, we are, at the same time, able to see that he can come out of these periods. And, on an even deeper level, both Jill and I come away from this experience realizing that we can deal with almost anything that Jordan's development might present us.

Jill, more than me, I must admit, manifests this determination in the face of our worst moments, not letting the spirit of the hour dictate what she is willing to try. When I, for example, suggest that Jordan's current behavior pattern makes our plans for a Florida vacation in December, 1990, an impossibility, she laughs it off, reminding me that I'm always expecting the worst. Her faith in herself never allows her or me, by association, to totally give up on bringing Jordan into a way of living as close to normal as possible. For six years, she has demonstrated this knack of showing her indomitable spirit at precisely the moment we need it to orient our way in a dark forest without trail markers. ❄

❄

❄

❄

❄ I'll return to that Christmas vacation in a moment. Now, though, I am traveling: spatially, east on route 2A from Acton to Lexington; and in time, back to my grandfather's little two-bedroom house in Pennsauken, New Jersey, in the mid-1950s. Physically, I am riding in the car on my way to work at Boston Higashi School on a pretty day in late winter. The sun is almost directly in front of me and low in the sky, so the visibility is poor. But my mind's eye senses the darkness of grandpop's living room at night. The family is huddled around the little television set. The lights have been turned off to minimize the distractions and improve our viewing of my grandfather's favorite show, "The Honeymooners." The glow from the small screen illuminates the acrid cloud of smoke coming from Pop's Camel cigarette—probably his fortieth of the day.

As the show's protagonist, Ralph Cramden, careens his way through another hair-brained scheme to escape his poverty and anonymity, my grandfather pays the homage of identity, laughing himself into a cough at the exploits. It's easy to see why Pop related so well to this character. Like Ralph, he too was "crammed in" to small living quarters, a dead-end job, and a permanent lack of recognition. And Ralph's plans to make it big or to impress the boss must have struck a respondent chord with his own failed attempts to better his fate. Incredibly, even in his 50s he would continue with his hopes and schemes.

What might have seemed astonishing to me then, becomes understandable when filtered through my own experience with autism. Ten, twenty, maybe a hundred disconfirming experiences with treatments for this crazy disorder aren't sufficient to kill the seed of hope within me. Just as there is for a weed sprouting through a crack in the pavement, there is always light to reach for. Today, and for several months since I first learned of it in an article in *The Harvard Educational Review* written by Syracuse University professor of special education Doug Biklen, "facilitated communication" has been that next flickering glimmer in the distance. Ironically, this hope comes at a time when we are about to give up on our long-term experiment with vitamin therapy, which has failed to deliver on its earlier promise. After about a year and a half of using the supplement, we have concluded that there

has been no appreciable improvement in Jordan's speech, behavior, or cognitive functioning.

Jill and I have spoken about facilitated communication,
and we have done some reading on the subject as well. At this
point, we are skeptical. The theory is that children with
autism have language but are unable to express it in a normal
way orally. Additionally—perhaps because they suffer from
apraxia—they are unable to direct their movements independently in order to use a typewriter or similar device
without assistance. But, according to those working with the
technique of facilitated communication, many of these people
have been able to produce highly intelligent communication
if someone supports their arm or wrist when typing. These researchers have also found that even very low-functioning,
non-verbal children have produced such communication.
Typically, these children are said to type statements such as "I
am not retarded" or "I want to go to a normal school."

Maybe it's possible. At one time Jordan knew his letters
and even some sight words. Somewhere in the dark recesses of
his mind this information may still survive. But is it likely? He
doesn't seem to suffer from apraxia; he would certainly be able
to pick out a small piece of candy from a large collection of
similarly shaped objects if given the opportunity, for instance.
Does it then make sense that he would be physically unable to
push the appropriate keys independently to spell words and
create messages if he had the mental capacity to do so? Well,
it could be that the task of communicating makes him so
anxious that he can't control his movements. Whatever the
likelihood, this prospect is too tantalizing to ignore, and, lucki-
ly, I will get an opportunity to see facilitated communication
for myself on this very day at Boston Higashi.

For some time, one of the students at the school has been
using facilitated communication at home. His parents have

been so impressed with the results that they have asked the school if they could sponsor a workshop for the staff. They are convinced that the school should investigate the possibilities of this method for their own child and others attending Higashi. The school has agreed to allow two trainers associated with Doug Biklen to conduct this staff development. An added bonus is that approximately fifteen students will be given the opportunity to communicate with these teachers on the Canon Communicator, a small typewriter-like device that is frequently used with this approach.

As I pull into Higashi's parking lot I have a tremendous feeling of anxiety. Even though I have felt that this idea has been oversold, I can't help wondering. After all, proponents of this technique are suggesting that not just a few, but most of the children they have worked with can communicate. Even a kid whose abilities have been dormant for over five years may succeed. When I think that Biklen's article appeared not in some "New Age Newsletter," but in *The Harvard Educational Review*, I wonder even more.

As the day progresses, I am outwardly busy with my job. Since I am not part of the teaching staff, I haven't really been invited to attend any of the sessions, and this enables me to keep my distance from the proceedings. At lunch, however, the trainers eat with the rest of the staff, and it's impossible to avoid them. They are reporting remarkable successes. They claim that the overwhelming majority of the children are communicating in a manner which would be nothing short of miraculous. The children's reported statements are amazingly similar to the kinds of communication that were attributed to children in the *Harvard Education Review* article, including claims about being able to read and think normally, despite being unable to express their thoughts in typical ways.

The American staff who witness this facilitated communication aren't as sanguine, however. Nobody reports that they could unequivocally establish that the children were communicating, and many are put off by the facilitators' heavy-handed hard sell. In fact, these facilitators seem to spend a good bit of the time at lunch prodding everyone with questions about how they see their method fitting in with the Higashi program. If the Americans appear less than convinced, one can almost see the thumbs-down sign in the eyes of the Japanese.

These sessions with the Higashi students do seem to convince one of the parents whose child participates. She comes away from the event absolutely certain that her child is communicating and later helps to organize workshops for other parents at the school, one of which Jill attends.

Meanwhile, I borrow one of the Canon Communicators that has been donated to the school to experiment with Jordan at home. We also try to interest Jordan in the keyboard of our computer and in identifying letters arranged on a sheet of paper—as they would be on a typewriter—to lend a little portability to our efforts.

For a period of about three weeks, Jill and I work with Jordan in this manner to see if we can elicit from him the kinds of communication that is being reported. The results are mixed at best. At times we think that he is able to identify the letters that form his name; or that he is able to locate the "y" or "n" to answer yes/no questions. He also seems to do better at identifying a specific picture from an array when we hold his hand. But mostly he rejects the whole concept. Coincidentally, he is going through a period when he is particularly tactilely defensive, and he often pulls away his hand and appears agitated when we try to pursue the matter.

Assuming that he is actually capable of communicating with us, our experience suggests that Jordan does not have a burning desire to do so. Moreover, the children whose parents claim they are communicating don't appear to be behaving any differently. The parents of one child who is facilitating claim that she now reads frequently and types such messages as "My mother isn't dedicated." But when I see her at school, she behaves as she always has, namely, jumping up and down and squealing. It seems a little unbelievable that children with little or no instruction in writing and reading have absorbed these skills. It seems even more incredible, however, that after demonstrating the ability to communicate they don't look or act differently.

To this writing, Jill and I see the potential of facilitated communication. Indeed, we have tried the method again and again with Jordan over the past few years. But we must be honest in reporting that it hasn't worked with Jordan. And claims of others that we have observed remain an unproven hypothesis.

Epilogue

*A*s I close this narrative, I think about the Christmas season of 1990, when we board that silver bird and head south, spending a week in the warm sunshine of the tropics and doing what the typical American tourists do. The highlight of our stay is the all-day trip to the Magic Kingdom.

At the end of a happy and busy day, we're sitting in the sky cable, riding high over the Disney complex. A full moon spreads its natural grace over the man-made marvels below. On the ground we see the throngs of people who have flocked here to the land of make-believe magic on this most enchanting of nights, New Year's Eve. My mind returns to the beginning of Jordan's life, when I thanked that invisible hand for placing me in the center of joy. At that time, I had a concrete vision of the good life as something of a place, like some magic kingdom that the fortunate few would be lucky enough to come upon, stocked with perennially happy loved ones, beautiful things, and wonderful experiences.

During the days when Jordan appeared normal, my life was like that place and like the snowflakes that fell on the day of his birth: beautiful, pristine, and unique. But the artificial state of the crystalline snowflake only exists within a narrow range of conditions which cannot persist. Jordan's demise took me out of that state and brought me into the rain—into a life of drab sameness that seemed unlivable. But rain is the reason we are able to live at all. It is the common experience of humanity. And no one escapes the sadness and suffering for which rain is often a symbol.

Even after I took that Alice in Wonderland plunge into the world of autism, I didn't immediately give up on my "snowflake" vision of the world. It took six years of wandering the labyrinth of my child's disorder to realize that the path to joy would lead back to me. I would come to understand through this trial that pinning my hopes for happiness on Jordan's recovery or on any particular outcome for my life was totally absurd. If the empyrean was to be found at all, it would be located deep within my self, in a core of acceptance and love of life, regardless of its outer dress.

The sky cable ride is almost finished when my daughter breaks into the final lines of a song from her most recent favorite movie: "If happy little blue birds fly, beyond the rainbow, why oh why can't I?" The ride and the song finish up at the same time.

> *"Does it hurt?" asked the Rabbit.*
>
> *"Sometimes," said the Skin Horse, for he was always truthful. "When you are Real, you don't mind being hurt."*
>
> *"Does it happen all at once, like being wound up," he asked, "or bit by bit?"*
>
> *"It doesn't happen all at once," said the Skin Horse. "You become. It takes time. That's why it doesn't often happen to people who break easily, or have sharp edges, or have to be carefully kept. Generally, by the time you are Real, most of your hair has been loved off, and your eyes drop out and you get loose in the joints and very shabby. But these things don't matter at all, because once you are Real, you can't be ugly, except to people who don't understand."*
>
> *The Velveteen Rabbit*
> *by Margery Williams* *

---

* Reprinted by permission of Running Press, 125 S. 22nd Street, Philadelphia, PA from *The Velveteen Rabbit* by Margery Williams, illustrated by Michael Green, copyright 1984 by Running Press.

About the author:

An elementary school assistant principal in Baltimore, Maryland, Craig Shulze has written on education for *The Baltimore Sun*, *The Evening Sun*, and *The Middlesex News* (Massachusetts). He holds a M. Ed. in Early Childhood Education from Towson State University, and a Ph.D. in Human Development from the University of Maryland. Craig and his wife, Jill, are former board members of the Baltimore Chapter of the Autism Society of America. The Schulze family lives in Silver Spring, Maryland.